I0081061

GOD…i believe
Simple Steps on the Path of Spiritual Christianity

by Branch Isole

1

GOD...i believe
by Branch Isole
Copyright © 2002, 2007
Revised and Reprinted 2007

Printed in the United States of America

Library of Congress Control Number: 2002114393
ISBN 0-9747692-0-7
(previously ISBN 1-591602-63-7)

All rights reserved. No part of this publication may be reproduced or transmitted in any form or by any means without written permission of the publisher.

All Scriptures taken from the Holy Bible, New International Version, Copyright © 1973, 1978, 1984, International Bible Society. Used by permission of Zondervan Bible Publishers.

To order additional copies

MANAO PUBLISHING
PO Box 1696
Lahaina, Maui, Hawaii 96767
www.manaopublishing.com

"Everything else can wait,
but the search for God cannot."

—*George Harrison, 1943–2001*

Table of Contents

Preface

Aloha! God has a secret and a blessing for you today.

Here's the secret: Each time and in every situation you find yourself, when you must decide or choose and you aren't sure what to do or how to react and respond, ask yourself:

• Will it be God's way or my way? and
• What Would Jesus Do?

Here's the blessing: If you ask these two questions, God will answer you. He will show you the way, He will direct your steps and He will advise you on how to respond.

Introduction

"It's the journey, not the destination."

Life is a journey with a destination. However, the question as important as to what and where the destination will be, is: What are the steps along the journey's path? It is in these steps that we experience pain and pleasure, trouble and elation, problems and profundities and the heartaches and blessings of life. Each journey is traveled on a path of priorities, decisions, choices, responses, actions and behaviors.

The world would like us to believe that we are what we possess: what it is, how much of it we control, how we acquired it, what it looks like and how we show it off in comparison to others. This is presented and perpetuated to us through endless commercial advertising of what we eat, drink, wear, drive, buy, sell, think and own; how and where we live and above all else, how much it all costs. For those who listen to the world, the destination is irrelevant. They puff up their chests and proclaim their mantra; "He (or she) who dies with the most toys wins."

For the believer of God's Word, the destination is already known and accepted, allowing the steps along the path to become the focus of the journey.

Spiritually, you are what you believe and how you use that belief to respond.

Everything is attitude, belief, and perception.

Attitude, belief and perception color everything we experience. Our attitudes, beliefs and perceptions determine our motivations and our actions. They help to shape each and every situation we find ourselves in and every decision or choice we make. Our attitudes, beliefs and perceptions influence what we each think, do and say. They reflect our expectations of what other people do and say, as well as how we respond to others and how they respond to us.

Exactly what are these three aspects? And how important or critical are they?

- *Attitude* is defined as "mental position or feeling with regard to a fact or state," "a manner showing one's feelings or thoughts," or "one's disposition or opinion."
- *Belief* is "trust or confidence" or the "conviction that certain things are true."
- *Perception* is an "awareness of one's environment through physical sensation" or "the mental grasp of objects through the senses; insight or intuition; knowledge understood by perceiving."

For a moment, close your eyes.
Take a deep breath and think back to any important experience in your life either positive or negative that

impacted you deeply, perhaps something at work or a personal relationship.

Now close your eyes again and reflect on the outcome or result of that experience.

And finally try to remember your attitude, belief or perception of that event or person during the moments when you were most heavily invested emotionally.

If in reflecting back to that particular experience you can now recall it differently with a more positive attitude, belief or perception, one of three things has happened:

1. you have grown as a result of that particular experience
2. you have matured in your life overall, or
3. you learned from that lesson of life and now approach similar situations and choices differently.

If however you are in the same place now as you were then, making the same decisions and choices and experiencing the same results over and over again, you are not growing and learning in your life. This situation represents a pragmatic definition of "emotional insanity" that is "repeating the same behaviors and expecting different results."

One of the goals on the path of our journey is to become free from this cycle of repetitive negative behavior. We must find the strength to stop making the same decisions, selecting the same choices and experiencing the same outcomes again and again while expecting different results (and making ourselves crazy along the way).

You may be saying "I've been there, done that and 'bought the whole darn wardrobe.'"

You may also be asking "Why do I keep doing this?" and "How can I break free?"

Jesus' answer: "Know the truth and the truth will set you free." [1]

You may or may not be aware of the immense impact that attitude, belief and perception have in your life. In this small book we will be looking at these three important aspects of life and the influences they exert upon our choices, decisions, actions and behaviors. For our purposes we will be focusing on these three attributes and the impact they have on us in connection with our spirituality.

Our life experiences demand that we respond by making priorities and choices and then by taking action. "Even not to decide is to decide." The decisions and choices we make based on our priorities of the moment determine our actions and responses. Each and every situation or event invariably comes down to one underlying and simple question that we must ask and answer repeatedly day after day. Believe it or not, it is the answer to this question that holds the key to your success, happiness, wealth and understanding. To find answers that may truly change your life and the circumstances you find yourself in, you are invited to read on.

Endnotes

All definitions herein are from *Merriam-Webster's Dictionary* (1997) or *Webster's New World Compact School Dictionary* (1994).

[1] John 8:32.

Part 1
Attitude

"Weakness of attitude becomes weakness
of character."
—*Albert Einstein, 1879–1955.*

CHAPTER 1

Worthiness vs. Unworthiness (Image vs. Ego)

One of the greatest challenges we face as we start a new relationship with the Lord is grappling with our feelings of unworthiness. It's in our misconception and limited knowledge of the Lord that we are often unsure as we wonder about His interest in us and our worthiness to be with Him. If we look closely we will find that our feelings of unworthiness are buried deep within the recesses of "self" somewhere between our over-inflated sense that we are good enough just as we are and the reality of our complacency level.

The sin of our human condition is evident by who we are and what we do, for in our world today most of us have no passionate longing for God. Therein exists both the subtlety and the power of sin and its manifestations in our over-indulgent selves.

Our "self" sins are part and parcel of our overtly indulgent twenty-first century vanity: self-righteousness, self-pity, self-confidence, self-sufficiency, self-admiration and self-love. The culminations of these "self" sins are the pinnacle of our society as seen in our egotism, exhibitionism and self-promotion.

Our selfishness is so much a part of our human nature, it fails to even come to our attention until one of the tragedies of our own self-importance corners and traps us.

For many of us it is only when we are tried and tested through our experiences of daily life that our sinful nature brings us face to face with our need for a relationship with God.

Just as there are conflicts between good and evil, between material and spiritual and between self and service, there is also a conflict between image and ego. We should remember that we have been made in God's image (character). What does this mean and how do we know what God is like? If we dare to explore and know the thoughts, words and deeds of Jesus Christ, [1] we will get a glimpse of God. [2]

Too often in our modern age we hear or read about a need to build up or bolster one's self-esteem or self-image. Let's look briefly at these two.

Self-esteem is defined as "belief in one's self" "undue pride in one's self" or "conceit." [3]

Self-image is described in the context of "one's concept of self" or "one's own abilities or worth."

Much of what we see in our hyper exposed world, filled with self-righteous cravings for our "fifteen minutes of fame" is actually ego, plain and simple. Although "ego" is defined as "the self," in the reality of today's world "EGO" often means "Edging God Out" of our lives rather than its dictionary definition: the "individual as self aware." By keeping God out of our lives we only deepen our feelings of unworthiness and our helpless emotion of "going it alone" in the world.

It is when we confuse our worth (character image) with our self-awareness (ego) that we find ourselves in difficulty. When we identify our self-image with the characteristics of God and emulate the thoughts, words and deeds of Jesus as our standard bearer for behavior, we will begin to understand the path to becoming more worthy of being in God's presence.

With a better understanding of this concept of "worthiness" let's look at the cycle we may find ourselves in and how we can become mired in our own behavior patterns and responses, which can keep us bound to our emotions of unworthiness.

Cycles, Lessons, and Insecurities

After a lifetime characterized by fits and starts, promises made and promises broken, putting our feet on a more righteous spiritual path and backsliding once again, we have finally had enough. We are ready for real change and decide to start fresh, giving ourselves over to a new relationship with the Lord.

However something happens to the new believer when he or she decides to take those steps toward a relationship with God.

Tests; small and large. Tests of faith. Tests of belief. Tests of patience. Tests of perseverance and Tests of surrender.

Do you remember a time when you managed to get yourself into a predicament and you made a promise to God? Perhaps it went something like, "I promise Lord, if you get me out of this one, I'll go to church every Sunday." Or perhaps you were willing to make some other arrangement, agreement or deal with God for his assistance out of your dilemma.

Well believe it or not, He heard you *and* He intervened for you! Did you uphold your end of the bargain? In many instances this type of dilemma or asking for relief from God and then not following through is what helps feed the sense of unworthiness within us. When we ask for help promising to repay in some way and then fail to abide by our word, we begin to feel more and more alienated and unworthy. We have let ourselves down by not fulfilling our part of the agreement.

God knows. Yes, He knows. And still after each broken promise God will continue to wait for us to once more take steps toward Him. Those steps will help us to develop a better understanding of Him and strengthen our feelings of worthiness. That's why each and every time throughout our lives when we call upon God; He is always ready for us to finally decide to fulfill our part of the covenant with Him.

God waits for us with open arms and compassionate love to come to Him and begin our walk as obedient children. [4] To start living anew.

Once we have invited the Lord into our lives and have decided to give ourselves over to new learning and new living, we are ready. Yes we're ready but ready for what?

Why, Blessings of course!

And what do we get? Tests, challenges, problems, troubles, trials and tribulations. We ask, "What in the world is this all about? I had these troubles before I came to God and I was coming to Him to be rid of them."

New tests and challenges come by accident, by circumstance, by the forces of evil or as in the Old Testament story of Job [5] sometimes even allowed by God Himself. Just as Job was challenged to exhibit his faithfulness, we too are challenged to show ours.

No matter their origin, our tests persist so that we might have additional opportunities to show the Lord that we fully intend to keep our feet on the path and become obedient listeners and practitioners of His Word. Will we fall away again, or stand firm when the next test comes?

We have chosen to live renewed with God. Now we must show Him that we are ready to do exactly that in all circumstances. Will we rely on conditions, circumstances and ourselves again or will we at long last relent, and depend upon God and His solutions? God's desire is to see if we are ready and willing to now remain faithful believers no matter what, so we are tested. Will we now believe His words and have the patience necessary to let His plan for us come to pass?

God wants to know if we will remain rock steady, grounded in His Word and our newly held beliefs. Or will we backslide again? God will uphold His promise and His part of the covenant. As always the real question is, will we be faithful this time?

Cycles, Lessons, and Insecurities (the How, the What, and the Why)

We often find ourselves in a cycle of despair and backsliding. It's a cycle that keeps us from breaking free and reinforces our feelings of unworthiness within. This cycle (the "how") is interconnected with two different but related aspects of our lives: the twelve lessons of life (the "what") and our insecurities (the "why").

Before going on we need to understand two important points. First, *all* people have and live with insecurities. We each have them. We have had them since childhood and our society and world feed upon and nurture them on a daily basis. And second, the lessons of life are common to each and every one of us. These lessons are active within each of our daily lives, circumstances and situations.

To make matters even more difficult it is not unusual to experience multiple events that embroil us in more than one lesson at a time, making our lives within the cycle even more complicated and seemingly out of control.

Let's look first at the progressive scenarios of this cycle of despair, in which we can find ourselves held hostage by our insecurities. Then we'll examine the "what" and the "why" and finally we'll see what it takes to break free and begin to live more successful and fulfilled lives.

Cycle (the How)

• **Scenario 1:** We are immersed in a struggle between our problems and our escape mechanisms. At this point in the cycle we are thinking only of our situations, our easiest remedies and ourselves. We move back and forth between the problem and our perceived solution of avoidance. At this stage we somehow believe that we are in control, even if our lives are totally out of control.

• **Scenario 2:** As we compound our problems through our escape mechanism responses and choices (drugs, sex, food, alcohol, shopping, etc.) we then begin the process of "beating ourselves up." In this way we can look for scapegoats or excuses upon which we can focus our energies as we self-inflict pain. We do not solve the problem and our escape mechanism behaviors do not provide resolutions.

• **Scenario 3:** We continue our downward spiral, going back and forth between our problems and our escape mechanisms. This only exacerbates our inability to cope, and ensures our continued backsliding and repetition of scenarios 1 and 2 of the cycle time and time again while beating ourselves up with more intent and intensity until we finally hit rock bottom.

• **Scenario 4:** We ask God for intervention in our lives.

• **Scenario 5:** We accept God's help but don't understand why He is not changing our entire life circumstances immediately so that we never have to experience these situations again.

• **Scenario 6:** We become impatient with God's inaction on our behalf, thus reinforcing and validating our self perceived unworthiness.

• **Scenario 7:** We have to make a choice. We will either obey God by changing our lives, enduring the testing and pain or we will backslide, retreating once again into the cycle at some point in scenarios 1–6. This is a cycle of behavior, responses and actions we may find ourselves in repetitiously.

How did we get here and more importantly, why?

Lessons (the What)

Let's first identify the "lessons of life" and then we'll look at our "life triangle." We all experience the lessons of life. They take place simultaneously or independently through our experiences with various people, places, things and events. They may come in isolation or in any combination, making our lives seem all the more confusing and frustrating. These are lessons by which we learn from and grow as part of our maturation process.

These are the lessons of life that we each encounter on a daily basis:

1. Insecurity
2. Responsibility
3. Reliability
4. Dependability
5. Accountability
6. Credibility
7. Risk
8. Trust
9. Commitment
10. Forgiveness
11. Truth
12. Love

We experience these lessons in different events and situations, at many times and in many ways during our lives either together or in isolation. For example at one moment you may be experiencing a situation that tests your "responsibility" response. At another time, your "commitment" and "reliability" may be tested by an event or an encounter with a particular person. You may experience any combination of lessons, which require attempts at response or resolution regarding any particular time, situation or event.

Imagine a juggler who is tossing and catching a chainsaw and is then thrown additional chainsaws until he or she is juggling five, then eight, then four and then one again in a constant ebb and flow. In our lives we are all jugglers. However we don't always know what circumstances will require us to juggle one or more of life's chainsaws. This begs the question of which is really in control, the juggler or the chainsaws? Of course, we (the jugglers) think that we are in control of our lives. As we juggle, we find ourselves enmeshed in the cycle described above trying to handle all the people, situations, decisions and choices associated with the lessons that require actions and responses from us each and every day.

The idea is to grow through each lesson to become more competent and successful. In this way we will not repeat the same inappropriate behavioral responses and actions, experience after experience, thus making ourselves emotionally crazy again.

Once we have successfully grown in our ability to respond to a particular lesson, each time thereafter when we are again tested by that lesson (i.e. responsibility), we now find we have the experience and confidence to handle that particular lesson effectively and will with success in the future. It is a terrific (and humbling) experience when we conquer one of our lessons. We are elated beyond words.

If you have seen the movie *"Rocky"* starring Sylvester Stallone, you may remember the scene when he ran to the top of the steps of the Philadelphia Museum of Art building as part of his conditioning regimen for his upcoming title fight with Apollo Creed. As with Rocky when we have conquered a lesson and finally reach the top of the steps, we raise our arms jubilantly and triumphantly in the air declaring our victory. This is the moment we have been waiting and working for. This is the moment of our dreams. It is at this moment that life congratulates us, pats us on the back and says "Great job."

As we beam and shine in our moment of glory, life leans over and whispers to us "OK, back to work. Now that you have conquered this lesson, it's time to tackle one of the others." As we are dragged back down the steps kicking and screaming not wanting to give up our euphoric sense of accomplishment, life invites us to take on another of the lessons by immediately presenting us with a new experience. Once again we are "thrown to the lions" of everyday living and to a different lesson, which we now need to address, attack and work on or through.

So, we have each of the lessons of life (the "what") being experienced as a situational problem within the cycle scenarios (the "how").

Here is an illustration of a personal struggle with a "lesson problem" in the cycle. (You may want to think of one from your own personal experience, present or past.)

Example

I am consistently late for work. As such I am shirking my responsibility to be punctual and on the job at the appointed and agreed upon time. If I am reprimanded for this behavior and refuse to take responsibility by blaming my tardiness on whatever excuse I can come up with, I am mired in my own inability or unwillingness to actually change my actions.

This is compounded when we are experiencing more than one lesson at a time. For example, if I am late for work (being irresponsible), that action directly affects my perceived value in terms of my reliability, dependability and credibility.

This is what our cycle looks like with this "lesson" added:

• **Scenario 1:** I am late for work again. It is from this point that I start my downward spiral in the cycle. My first battle is experiencing the emotion of guilt over my excuse given in response to the reprimand I received for failing to be on time. This feeds my feelings of embarrassment, shame and unworthiness. I turn to my remedy, my personal escape mechanism: drugs, sex, alcohol, food, yelling at my wife or kicking my dog.

Whatever my sin, vice or remedy may be, I justify, validate or feel better about what has happened as I am again faced with my problem.

This will invariably precipitate additional problems or troubles. Many of these I may be familiar with, having been in the cycle before.

• **Scenario 2:** Initially I go back and forth between my problem (being late for work) and my remedy (overeating to feel better about my failure to take responsibility). In this part of the cycle I come to a point when I realize that I am unhealthy. In denial, I tell myself "The boss is always on me because I am too fat" and I begin the process of beating myself up over the cause and effect of my behavior.

At this point, I'm trapped between wallowing in feelings of unworthiness and failure and taking solace in my escape mechanisms. Going back and forth between these two, I may find myself repeating this scenario over and over again in response to scenario one.

• **Scenario 3:** I continue to go from my problem to my remedy to self-criticism. I also continue to reinforce the sense that I am unworthy as the cycle increases and intensify. As I start to reach bottom I must find a way out and a solution. It is at this stage that I again try dieting or some other program, knowing full well that I have failed before in this same situation. Finally having nowhere else to turn I cry out to, or someone suggests that I "try God."

• **Scenario 4:** They say "Try God! He cares about you and He loves you!" So I finally decide to turn to God after all. I ask myself "How can it hurt? I can't be any worse off than I am already." The problem is I have asked Him before and each time when He helped me, I only remembered Him until I was late for work again. After that it was back to "business as usual." I have asked God to come into my life and help me but I think to myself, "Why should He? I am not worth it."

This mindset allows me to continue to beat myself up even more. After all hasn't God been there for me time and time again in the past, but when all was said and done, all I did was turn my back on Him again and return to my old comfortable ways?

We each might ask, "How could He possibly be interested in me? I am so unworthy of His love and attention." Not only are we unlovable in our own eyes, but now even God Himself cannot possibly love us.

• **Scenario 5:** I am in scenario 4 and decide that I will embrace God and begin to try. I turn to Him and just as He has done before, He intervenes in my life and problem.

As believers, every time we ask God for help, He will in fact intervene on our behalf.[6] When we accept Him and our immediate troubles subside, we are rewarded with a peace that begins to help us finally get on track. Unfortunately the one thing we discover when we are depending on God is that He and we are often on different time schedules. [7] He has much more patience than we do. The peace He brings and the patience He requires are sometimes more than we think we can bear. Yes we get a reprieve from our troubles but we become impatient, expecting our lives to be turned around immediately.

We may say "I turned to Him and He answered my prayers but now what? What do I do next?" So we turn away from God. "He seems to be somewhere else anyway and not really in my life after all." And back to our old ways we slide, while telling others and ourselves "I'm not really a religious person anyway" or "I'm OK now."

• **Scenario 6:** Instead of simply leaving God again (as in scenario 5) I have spiraled so far down that I decide to really stick it out and try to give Him more of myself.

What we often find when we have made this commitment is that we are soon bombarded with new trials, tests and conflicts. "Why is this happening?" we ask. "I have given myself over to the Lord and now even more difficulty is happening in my life!" As new believers, we find ourselves struggling against new or greater odds.

With disgust and exasperation we finally declare "See, I told you I was unworthy and unlovable" and back to our old ways we go with a vengeance. We may find ourselves trapped in the cycle at any point and in any scenario, repeating steps endlessly.

• **Scenario 7:** Will it be "God's way or my way"? We have been through the cycle so many times that we finally reach a point where we realize to walk our path according to God's plan will require time, patience, trust, belief and a lasting effort. He has answered us, aided us, helped us and saved us from both the world and ourselves time and time again. Now it is time for us to face every new situation knowing that we have a choice to make *each time* we are tested or tempted. "Which way will I go? Which path will I choose?"

We have discovered that we can't do it on our own. And we can no longer do it the world's way. We must trust our faith, our belief and our past experiences that have brought us to this point. Now we must stand firm with the knowledge and presence of God in our lives. It may not make things any easier or immediately different but at least we now know that we won't be facing our tests, trials and tribulations alone. What we finally realize and understand is; turning to God is *not* a one-time action. It is an everyday living experience, one that is repeated in multiple situations over and over again each day. Sounds easy when we finally get to that end point in scenario 7, doesn't it?

But what about these tests? Believe it or not even when we have finally surrendered, our problems and troubles may not be over. [8] In fact it is at this point that we may experience even more trials and tribulations. "How can this be?" the new believer asks. We should take a moment to talk about three areas.

Our troubles and problems and our escapes (temptations, vices and sin filled or inappropriate behavior) work hand in hand no matter which scenario we find ourselves in. As long as we are caught up in, and are operating between these two (our problems and our escape mechanisms) the cycle is inescapable.

As long as we continue to beat ourselves up whether it pertains to the past or the present, we have little chance of breaking the cycle (again no matter which scenario we are in).

When we finally surrender, inviting God into our lives, agree to follow Him and turn our daily struggles over to Him, this time often becomes our biggest test of all.

Tests of our belief and faith in God come throughout life whether we believe or not. Tests, trials and tribulation can come in three ways: (1) by accident or circumstance (2) by the forces of evil or (3) by God's allowance. No matter where they may come from we must remember that all experiences test our belief, faith and commitment. For the professed new Christian or the neophyte believer who has finally accepted the presence of the Lord within his or her life and is now turning to God for guidance and relief, oftentimes our struggles intensify. Why is this?

Why would God test us or allow us to experience accidents or to fall prey to Satan? [9] The answer is really quite simple. After all of our backsliding, God wants to know if this time we are really going to trust and believe in Him, His power and His Word. What we discover when we have made our commitment to God is that regardless of our old troubles that may persist or any new ones we might encounter, He is true to His Word. The real question is, are we going "stick it out" with God this time or are we going to stumble and fall again when the pressure and heat is turned up?

It's amazing how as Christians or new believers we may be tested in new ways as never before, sometimes even more than when we struggled on our own. God wants to see if this time we are truly ready to surrender to Him and trust in His Word.

Now the big question: Why are we stuck in this cycle (scenarios 1–6) over and over again? The answer: our insecurities.

Insecurity (the Why)

When we are secure with who we are, we have more balance in our lives with other people, places and things and are less focused on our provincial interests. A security within allows and encourages us to be in a place of higher, selfless consciousness in our actions and responses.

As we experience the lessons of life, our insecurities hamper our abilities to grow confidently in who we are. When we are insecure we are constantly worried about who we *are not* and become heavily invested in our appearance to others. We constantly worry and ask "Will I measure up to what others may think of me?"

This is because we live in an age of pretense. We can never totally relax for we live with secret fears that someday we will be found out. The career person fears failures and foibles in the face of peer pressure. The well heeled traveler fears that he or she will meet another who has been to more places and has seen more attractions. The well educated person may fear being in the presence of one with a "higher degree" and the rich may reel under the pressure of being compared in such a way that their possessions will appear cheap or inadequate when contrasted to another's. The greater our insecurities the more easily worried or paranoid we become about how we will be perceived by others in every situation.

Here is a graphic that may help us to better understand the lessons and their relativity in our lives:

GOD

```
            Love
            Truth
         Forgiveness
         Commitment
            Trust
            Risk
          Credibility
        Accountability
         Dependability
          Reliability
         Responsibility
```

Insecurity

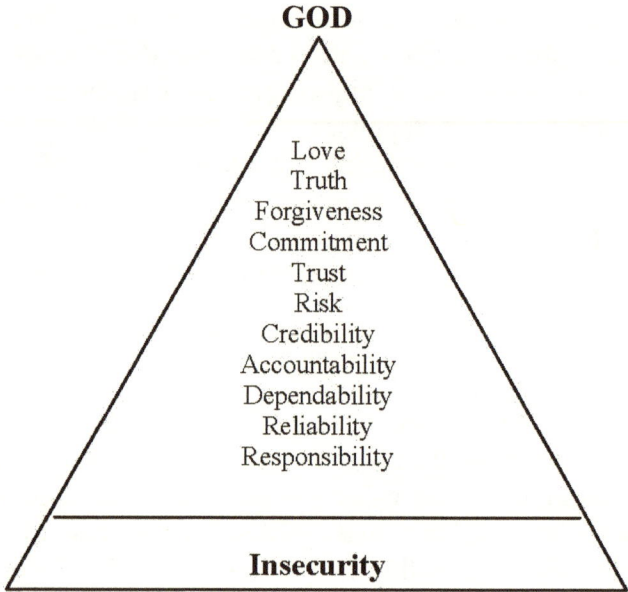

It is in living these lessons of life that we find our opportunities to grow and mature. These are the twelve lessons that we each experience and are applicable to each and every situation in our lives.

In each experience you have, you are coping with, struggling with or effectively handling one or more of these lessons.

You'll notice that in our triangle, lesson 1 (our base and largest part) is our "insecurity." Insecurity is life's fundamental lesson. We all start in this lesson of insecurity. Each person must overcome his or her insecurities to grow effectively and successfully through each of the other lessons.

Although there is a certain amount of comfort in

staying in this place of insecurity we know so well, as long as we are there we will be unable to grow and move forward in our lives. The "I" within us represents our insecurities, as in: "I need, I want, I should have, I should get, I am too bald, too fat, too short or I am not pretty enough, rich enough, thin enough or sexy enough."

Furthermore our insecurities force us to face two big questions in each and every situation we find ourselves: "What if I am rejected?" and "What if I fail?"

It is the emotion of self-pity (our "poor me" attitude) hidden deep within these two questions that keep us locked within their grasp and seduces us as submissive victims of our own insecurities. Our behaviors keep us stuck at this level as we face many instances when our actions are not as they should be. That is, not being or doing our best because we use our insecurities as excuses for our behavior, which keeps us from growing. This can become evident in our relationships, both personal and occupational as we grow into adulthood believing that our worthiness is dependent upon how others perceive us.

When we are focused on the "I" of our insecurities, we are in a continual struggle with ourselves. We constantly wonder subconsciously, "How am I going to face the people I know, if I fail or I am rejected?" As long as we are operating in and on this base level of insecurity, we will wrestle with ourselves as noted above "I need this, I want that, I should have this, I should get that, I deserve this" or,

"I am too 'whatever.'"

"I am not pretty enough, handsome enough, rich enough, tan enough, thin enough" etc. or whatever our personal demon may be. The major problem is with our insecurities so profound; we tend to have multiple troubles when faced by one or more of the other lessons.

The instruments and vehicles of instant world wide communication continually play upon us and to our desires as we aspire to appear to be whom and what we are not.

We think that those whom the media constantly bombard us with; the rich, the famous and the glamorous of our world are perfect and happy. We are enticed to be more like the famous or infamous. We buy into the belief that to be happy with ourselves, we must be more like the celebrities whose lives we are shown. They all seem to be so perfect, so happy, so "in touch and in control." We are forever aspiring to be as wealthy as Bill Gates, as popular as Britney Spears, as famous as Michael Jordan, or as infamous as Osama Bin Laden. Today this condition has been elevated as never before and permeates our entire way of life, appealing to our incessant desires and our need to be recognized.

Cash, clothes, cars, cosmetics and all the other commodities of our world are available to be presented and sold to us twenty-four hours a day, seven days a week. Advertising is the lifeblood of this artificiality and as long as we buy into the hype, we will continue to find that we don't and won't measure up. We will continue to be insecure about our lives and ourselves. The truth of the matter is, you are and can only be who you are.

Let's look at how we can grow through our insecurities.

We must overcome and grow through this lesson of insecurity or we will be plagued with problems and troubles throughout life. Whenever we face situations that require our response, we can go to several different places.

If we handle a situation successfully, we keep growing and moving forward. We experience personal growth not only as it applies to a particular lesson but also as to our confidence and strength, which are more easily transferred to other situations and lessons.

If however we are not successful, we may have a tendency to try and placate our inadequacies, failures or rejections within a particular situation by retreating again into our insecurities. In doing so we have the chance to blame our inadequacies on the outcome or on our inability to cope as it relates to our insecurities (I blame it on my weight). We can dwell in our insecurities and proceed to go to wherever we find comfort. Often this will be within the realm of our escape mechanisms, vices, sins or other inappropriate behaviors. It could also be where we simply beat ourselves up again and again. If we retreat to any of these, we are likely to begin the downward spin and repetitive cycle that we are already familiar with from having "been there and done that."

These daily battles will keep us mired in and struggling with our lesson of insecurity. Everything we deal with or everything we try is couched in the moment as we compare ourselves to someone or something else. If we fail in a particular moment we may think we are doomed. This struggle within the lesson of insecurity is very damaging and dangerous for it keeps us from growing. We are not only failing to grow through the lesson of insecurity, we are also kept from successfully growing through the other eleven lessons of life as well. This is because as long as we are trapped in and by our insecurities it remains difficult to free ourselves and to grow through any of the other lessons. This is especially true if we are trying to juggle situations, people and events from the other lessons, which most often is the case.

Remember that all of the lessons are happening to us all the time, in any order and possibly in multiples of simultaneous people and events. We may become stuck in our insecurities and unable to extricate ourselves. This lesson is the most important to overcome for it gives a safe haven each and every time we can't, or we refuse to grow. Each time we have troubles, problems, failures or rejections in any of our lessons, our insecurities allow us a refuge to where we can go instead of facing our demons head on. It also gives us a place where we can beat ourselves up when we fail or when we are rejected in any of the other lessons we face. As long as we are trapped in our insecurities, we will have difficulties growing successfully in any area, endeavor or arena.

We must learn to be OK with our imperfections.

Having examined insecurity, which is the lesson we struggle with the most, let's look at the others by adding three new aspects, for there are several interesting anomalies here. First you'll notice that lessons 2–6 are more pragmatic in nature, while 8–12 are more esoteric. Also lessons 2–6 tend to be more male dominant, whereas 8–12 are usually more female oriented in their applications and presence. Traditionally males tend to spend more time and energy in lessons 2–6 becoming more accomplished at worldly (usually career) applications. As such men often have more difficulty expressing themselves in lessons 8–12 while the opposite may be true for many females. The third aspect of the lessons is that they each hold a different defined application in action. As an independent experience, each teaches a necessary facet to be learned and accomplished as part of the whole of living.

Lesson 7 (Risk) is general in nature and applies to all of us indiscriminately. To illustrate this, we have superimposed them onto our triangle:

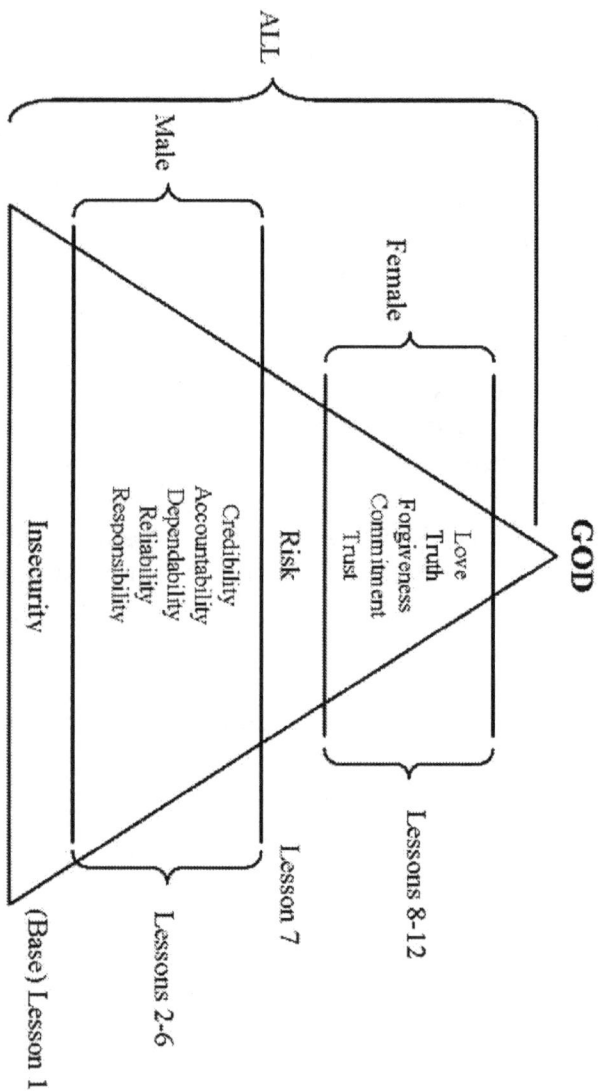

ALL

Male

Female

GOD

Love
Truth
Forgiveness
Commitment
Trust

Risk

Credibility
Accountability
Dependability
Reliability
Responsibility

Insecurity

Lessons 8-12

Lesson 7

Lessons 2-6

(Base) Lesson 1

How do we gain confidence within each lesson, which will then allow us to no longer struggle each time an event or experience takes place within a given lesson of our lives? We must overcome our insecurities. We do this by:

1. Becoming more and more confident in who we are, as we are.
2. Not repeating inappropriate behavior resulting from poor choices and decisions.
3. Surrendering our "perceived" control of each situation to the Lord (scenario 7 of our cycle).
4. Knowing that God will not abandon us, ever.
5. Building upon our successes, knowing that we won't abandon Him (or ourselves) again.

How can you experience and see this growth as you gain balance and confidence? As you become more secure with yourself as an individual, you will learn from your successes *and* your failures, as you turn to the Lord. The Lord will answer if you will ask, and He will show you the way, if you believe. [10]

Remember our "*Rocky*" steps of victory? Each time you are successful with a lesson, life briefly congratulates you and then just as quickly throws at you from one of your other lessons, a new and different opportunity to try your hand at one you have yet to master. By doing two things you can ensure that you are continuously and successfully growing. First, with each lesson (test, temptation, trial or tribulation) you may now apply your previous and successful applications. Second, you now look to the Lord for strength and guidance for a new or better solution that will work with any new lesson or problem.

At this point you will be ready to tackle any lesson, situation or event you may face. With confidence you are prepared to face all that life may throw at you whether in isolation or in combination. If you try and fail, you no longer need to retreat into your old insecure self. Now when you are facing problem situations, you confidently look for solutions instead of dwelling on the trouble, pain and potential negative outcomes. As such even if you come up with a solution that doesn't work you are one step closer to finding one that does and now, you confidently know of one that doesn't. You won't keep making yourself crazy by repeating the same mistake or behavior over and over again while expecting a different result. When you now face a problem and find a successful solution that works, you can apply that solution to every similar problem that may come your way. This is growth in action.

So what does all this mean to you and how do you successfully keep growing?

Understand that God is at the apex of our "lessons of life triangle." It is where He is and where we aspire to be. We are intent on working our way through the various lessons so we may experience more truth and love in our lives, for they complete us and make us whole. For the Christian the idea is to come closer to God, to become a more complete and more obedient "child of God" [11] and to become more Christ-like in our behavior. [12] God helps us to see that our imperfections are not only normal, but they also represent the necessity of a relationship with Him and His Son to successfully grow and stop the downward spiral of life's cycle of failure and despair. God shows us how to break the ties that bind us so that we may finally begin to grow and become healthier with His love and guidance. Our aim is to master the lessons and to be our highest loving selves at all times and in all conditions or situations. In this way each time you are faced with an opportunity to respond or react within each lesson, you have the keys necessary for successful living in that moment.

Having said all this, what is the quickest way to solve the problems that may plague you through and within all the twelve lessons of life? The answer: turn your triangle upside down!

Go to God first! Begin with God. Have a living relationship with God. Come from your highest loving self and work through each lesson coming from a base of love and truth, instead of insecurity.

Endnotes

[1] John 8:19: "If you knew me, you would know my Father also."

[2] John 14:9: "Anyone who has seen me has seen the Father."

[3] All definitions are from *Merriam-Webster's Dictionary* (1997) or *Webster's New World Compact School Dictionary* (1994).

[4] 2 John 6: "And this is love: that we walk in obedience to his commands."

[5] Job 2:10: "Shall we accept good from God, and not trouble?"

[6] John 15:7: "If you remain in me and my words remain in you, ask whatever you wish, and it will be given you."

[7] 2 Peter 3:9: "The Lord is not slow in keeping his promise, as some understand slowness. He is patient with you."

[8] Matthew 6:34: "Each day has enough trouble of its own."

[9] Job 1:7–12: "The Lord said to Satan, 'Where have you come from?' Satan answered the Lord, 'From roaming through the earth and going back and forth in it.' Then the Lord said to Satan, 'Have you considered my servant Job? There is no one on earth like him; he is blameless and upright, a man who fears God and shuns evil.' 'Does Job fear God for nothing?' Satan replied. 'Have you not put a hedge around him and his household and everything he has? . . . But stretch out your hand and strike everything he has, and he will surely curse you to your face.' The Lord said to Satan, 'Very well, then, everything he has is in your hands, but on the man himself do not lay a finger.'"

[10] 1 John 5:14–15: "This is the confidence we have in approaching God: that if we ask anything according to his will, he hears us. And if we know that He hears us—whatever we ask—we know that we have what we asked of him."

[11] 1 John 3:1: "How great is the love the Father has lavished on us, that we should be called children of God!"

[12] Philippians 2:5: "Your attitude should be the same as that of Christ Jesus."

CHAPTER 2

Surrender
(Conscience, Conflict
and Control)

Conscience

Surrender. What a terrible word. What an obnoxious thought. What an alien concept this has become in our world today. Everywhere we look we see images and examples of people who refuse to surrender, to give in or to even entertain the thought.

They are our heroes and our desire is to be like them. We might ask ourselves "Why should we give up control?" Our favorite celebrities don't surrender and look at how rich and famous they are. Our politicians don't surrender and look how powerful they are. They'll do whatever it takes to win election and re-election or to gain and control the power. Why should we give in? Our sports idols don't surrender because winning and being "number one" are everything. Our business icons never surrender. They buy and sell to turn large profits regardless of what it may do to their companies, industries or employees. No one we know is ever willing to surrender, not even us. How in the world can we be in control of our lives and get all the things we want if we are willing to surrender?

It's not the American way. And after all, doesn't everyone want to be like us?

If we look at stories in the Old Testament books of the Bible we discover a history of the Hebrew patriarchs and the Israelites. This history has a repetitive theme: rejection of God and His Word results in troubles on one hand, and surrender to God and His Word results in blessings on the other hand. When people are disobedient to God they "reap what they sow." When these same people are obedient to the Lord, they also reap what they sow; however they reap blessings in circumstance after circumstance.

There is a pattern here, do you see it?

Look at biblical stories, look at scripture, look at history, look around you and look in the mirror. Whoever and wherever we are, when we are obedient to the Word of God, we are blessed. When we are ignorant, defiant or disobedient to His Word we suffer the consequences of our own making and choices. It's that simple.

Why do we suffer? We refuse to listen, we refuse to learn or we refuse to surrender. We will continue to repeat the same inappropriate behavior again and again regardless of, or in some instances because we already know the outcome.

For many of us through our incessant need and desire to be in control we find ourselves comfortable in the repetitive misery of our actions. It is far more frightening to even consider the possibilities of believing, breaking free, being alone and on our own, than heaven forbid; wrong in the eyes of the world. How can we possibly prove ourselves to all those people who are watching us if we aren't in total control?

Conflict

Let me ask you a question: How do we inherently know right from wrong?

Why is it when a young child steals he or she experiences the emotions of dread and guilt?

Why do we lie when confronted with the truth? We commit the act and feel the guilt, but tell ourselves, "everyone else does it" or "I deserve it" so we can feel better and excuse our own actions.

Why do so many rules, regulations, laws, codes and codicils govern everything in life from A to Z? And why are all these rules are so easy to break?

From the moment of birth, we are imbued with the essence of God's spirit within us in the form of a conscience.[1] It is our conscience with which we struggle in every situation when we must choose between appropriate and inappropriate behavior..

From our earliest opportunities we ask ourselves "In this instance, do I follow my conscience or do what I want?" It is from our earliest days that we come into conflict with our conscience and thus are we in conflict with God.

Are you in control of your possessions or are they in control of you? Nowhere are our conflicts more evident and real than in the collection and display of our possessions. "Things" were intended for us to have and to use, but only for our external needs. In human history "things" were initially the rudimentary tools and implements essential for survival against animals and the forces of nature. Through millennial progression with ever advancing technology, most of us now find all of our essential needs for survival being adequately met. Our world also provides us with more free and leisure time than ever before along with a myriad of possessions to have, use and control. We grow up and are socialized thinking that the more possessions we have the happier and more fulfilled we will be. For many today however, we may be finding that our possessions actually own and control us.

Possessions and "things" will never fill the internal void within you. You don't believe it? Ask someone who is extremely wealthy. If he is brutally honest he will tell you that his material possessions make life more comfortable but nothing he has can satisfy the essential longings of life.

This is where and how our true spiritual troubles start. And troubles within must, and always will manifest themselves without. There is nowhere to run, no way to hide and no suppression of your troubles. Sooner or later your problems will find an escape route and just as your possessions are external, so too will be your pain. Deep within our hearts, where emptiness turns into the real pain of our lives, our desires can be satisfied only by a relationship with God. As George Harrison expressed, "Everything else can wait, but the search for God cannot."

It is important that we take a moment to identify a caveat concerning wealth. The Lord does not want you to struggle in poverty. Nowhere in the Bible does God say that He wants you to be financially poor or destitute. In fact just the opposite is true.

If you look back at many biblical stories and histories, you will find that many of the people with whom God had direct contact and covenants were wealthy by the standards of their day and through obedience to God became even wealthier. Likewise some of those who had little but were faithful also ended up with great riches. God wants each of us to prosper and become good stewards of the possessions in our lives.

People often quote (misquote, really) the Bible by saying "Money is the root of all evil." I say "misquote," because the scripture is actually, "For the *love of money* is a root of all kinds of evil."[2] When money and possessions become the desires of our hearts, the idols to which we covet, honor and bow and the be all and end all of our existence, our troubles truly begin. The Bible tells us succinctly, "You cannot serve both God and Money."[3] "Either

51

you will hate the one and love the other, or you will be devoted to the one and despise the other."[4]

What are we being told here? Simply this: God wants you to be wealthy and blessed in all ways. He also wants you to realize and recognize where those opportunities and blessings come from. God wants you to have much, but He also wants you to be judicious with what you have and how you manage it. And, He wants you to share your blessings with those who have little. Where there is a need, fill it and you will know the true meaning of the words "It is more blessed to give than to receive."[5]

If you truly want more, give more. If you truly want to have blessings in your life, remember and recognize the one from whom all those blessings come. If you truly wish to experience everything that life has to offer, make God the Lord of your heart, not "things."

For many of us today "things" have taken over our hearts. For many of us, our possessions express our true nature. For many their identity is found in anything and everything material. Our love of "things" has grown within us like a viral cancer. It has become part of our nature and our identity to possess more and more. We covet "things" more passionately than passion itself. We strut around our world with our chests puffed out proudly stating that these "things" are "mine." Today the words "me," "my" and "mine" describe attitudes, beliefs and perceptions that are symptomatic of our disease. This cancer of possessiveness grows and flourishes within us like a rampant virus and we dare not excise even a portion of it or surely our identity will die.

"Things" now represent necessity to us and we will do whatever it takes to ensure that we continue to possess more. Our current selfishness and need to possess are found in the Wall Street words of our world: "gain" and "profit." Our thoughts of material gain need to be tempered by Jesus' words: "What good is it for a man to gain the whole world, yet forfeit his soul?"[6]

Life was never intended to be this way. No wonder we experience such problems and turmoil when we have little and even more when we have much. God's gifts have not taken His place in our hearts and lives but our lust for them has. The nature of our lives has been turned upside down because of our desire for "things" instead of the one who has provided them.

How different our lives would be if our thoughts were on life itself when we awoke each morning instead of on monetary profit and material gain. It is not our possessions that have condemned us; it is making them our heart's desire that has.

It is our insatiable selfish desire for additional gain that continues to keep us from Him. Like the fallen angels we too experience distance and separation from God.

The Old Testament story of Abraham and his son Isaac[7] gives us a dramatic glimpse of possessions and a surrendered life. Abraham was old enough to have been Isaac's great-grandfather when the infant was born and Isaac immediately became the apple of his father's eye and the delight of his heart. From the first moment that Abraham saw the tiny child he became an eager love slave of his second son. Years later when Isaac was only a boy God instructed Abraham "Take your son, your only son Isaac whom you love and go to the region of Moriah. Sacrifice him there as a burnt offering on one of the mountains I will tell you about."[8] This was to be Abraham's "trial by fire." God had instructed Abraham to kill his own son.

To kill his own son.

Not until Jesus' moment of truth in the Garden of Gethsemane[9] when He wrestled with His own humanity and God's plan for him, would such a painful decision be experienced and such a loving choice be made.

You and I, the rich and the poor, the mighty and the lowly, those chosen by and spoken to by God, even God's own Son, are all destined to face trials of trust, faith and belief.

With the altar preparations made and Isaac's sacrificial body bound and tied into position, Abraham held the killing knife in his hand. As the old man slowly began to lift the blade over his head ready to strike the final blow and pierce Isaac's heart, God stopped him saying "Do not lay a hand on the boy. . . . Do not do anything to him. Now I know that you fear God because you have not withheld from me your son, your only son."[10]

God could have worked at the outer edges of Abraham's life but He always works from the inside out. God's way is to cut to the quick to the heart of the matter having it over and done with in one swift act of decision, surrender and separation.

After so many years of covenant God wished to remain the unchallenged focus of Abraham's heart. God wanted to remove from Abraham his overwhelming desire for Isaac above all else. The Lord wanted to correct Abraham's substitution of love that now existed in his heart for his son Isaac. Abraham had put the desire of his entire being into his love for his son Isaac, and now God had taken it from him. Now Abraham was truly a surrendered man, a totally obedient man, a man who possessed nothing. From that moment on his worldly goods and possessions meant nothing to him.

Here is the spiritual secret of God's lesson for Abraham and for us. The words "me" "my" and "mine" no longer existed for Abraham. He could not explain it to anyone but the sense of possession was gone from his heart. All "things" had now become solely external. The people of his world saw Abraham as being wealthier than all others in goods and possessions but now he himself knew the truth: he realized that he owned nothing for now his real treasures were inward and eternal. His heart was free at last to serve God.

The steps of the process leading up to that moment of truth for Abraham had been excruciatingly bitter but they were exacting in their effect. It was in this way that God tested Abraham. He attempts to do the same with us.

When we realize this statement to be true and the gravity of it in our lives we face two challenges just as Abraham did. First, we will understand surrendering to the Lord only through our own experiences. And second, our acts of surrender will come to us only as we are tested. Being tested we may face harsh and bitter experiences that will seem to pierce our hearts and tear at our souls. And as we have already experienced in our own lives, we may never know when, where or what our next test will be or look like.

Undoubtedly for each test, decisions will need to be made and your future will depend upon your choices. God allows us to experience all of the tests, temptations, troubles, trials, tribulations and lessons so that we will at long last turn to Him, invite Him into our lives and begin to truly live heart-to-heart with Him.

All that we are, all that we have and all that we are willing to commit to the Lord are in truly good and safe hands. When God dwells in that sacred place of your heart, where your "things" now live, you too will know and experience the treasure of blessings.

Our possessive clinging to things and people often hinders us from surrendering to the Lord. This is especially true when we experience the pain and loss of a relative or friend to death. However as believers, we have nothing to fear, not even death for God sent His Son to save, not to destroy. When you face your next test ask yourself "Where is my heart?" Once the heart is truly committed to something; good, bad or ugly, the mind and body will follow.

God wants you to come to Him from and with your heart, plain and simple. The Lord wishes to dwell spiritually with you. It's what He wants from you, from each of us. It has been this way since the beginning and will be this way until the end.

Control

Like so many other aspects of life today this idea of "surrender" leaves us with a feeling of impending loss. We think the way to ensure that we will not face or feel this loss is to make certain we are always in control.

I'd like to ask you a question: Who is in control of your life? You? Your boyfriend or girlfriend? Your boss? Your spouse? Your parents? Your church? The advertising sellers, peddlers and purveyors of American commerce?

It is we who keep ourselves bound and tied. We have been taught to think that the more control we have in our lives the happier and more successful we will be. This is reinforced daily from many different sources. The truth is the more you believe that you are in control the easier it is for your doubts, fears and insecurities to hold you, as you try to live up to the perceived expectations of others. We give in to the very people who want us to believe that we are in control while they lead us to where they want us to be. As long as you think you are in control, you never will be. You will always be striving to live according to someone else's standards or desires.

If you are not in control when you think you are and you fear giving up your control by surrendering, but you are trapped if you don't surrender, what are you to do?

Here is an example of this concept of control and surrender in action.

In the days of the first century throughout the Roman Empire the movement of soldiers was necessary and constant. One of the duties of the Roman legions was to travel, guard and protect the extensive road system of the empire. This meant great movements of men and their goods. Any Roman soldier could conscript anyone who was not a citizen of Rome to carry his belongings for a distance of one mile. This practice caused much disgust, disdain and disrespect for Roman soldiers among the local populace.

In addressing this issue Jesus told His listeners to do something which to them, was even more confusing. He told them "If someone forces you to go one mile, go with him two miles."[11]

Now why would He say this?

When a non-citizen was ordered to carry a soldier's belongings, the soldier was in control. By going the extra mile, the person who had been forced into conscription now established not only the situational positioning but more importantly regained his dignity. The power of the psychological advantage of the soldier and the obligation of the non-citizen was neutralized with the second mile. Going the extra mile may be seen by some as giving in or surrendering but any time we serve of our own free will we are not only regaining the control over our own actions but whether it is acknowledged or not we may gain another's respect.

Believe it or not we are always exactly where we want to be and we always get exactly what we want. Now many may disagree with this but it is true. The choices we make determine where we are and what we get out of life. Once we have decided in the depths of our hearts that no power can stop us, nothing will. Not even God Himself.

Through His awesome love and understanding God has given us the free will to decide our own choices in our own ways and on our own paths. He has no interest in forcing your decisions and choices. When you finally decide to come to Him, He wants it to be of your own free will. The Lord wants you to be in a relationship with Him because that is where you want to be and what you truly want to experience. God wants it to be your committed heart that leads you to Him. In this way He knows you will stay. When your decisions and choices are made of your own free will and you take responsibility for your own actions you may freely surrender control of your life to God and yet never feel the burden of loss again. Perhaps you have heard the statement "Let go and let God." When you "let go" of your troubles and problems and give them over to the Lord, an answer will be given to you. The control is now in the proper hands. Your conflict will become non-existent and your conscience will be clear.

The only control you truly have is over your own responses, actions and behaviors to the situations and events you experience. Everything else is trying to drown you in a whirlpool of misunderstanding and deception. The "Seven Deadly Sins:" Pride, Greed, Lust, Anger, Laziness, Resentment, and Excess have caused more human heartache and pain than all the diseases that have ever plagued, ravaged or afflicted us.

Your path may be rocky but the one sure way to smooth out the journey is to surrender. And therein lies the conflict between your conscience and you, the inner fight for control.

Let go of the control. Trust the Holy Spirit of God within you or trust your conscience. Ask yourself the Lord's two questions when you face conflict: Will it be God's way or my way? and, What would Jesus do? By asking these questions, you will get answers and the differences you experience will be as wide and deep as life and death.

Go ahead, "let go and let God" and start living!

Endnotes

[1] Hebrews 13:20–21: "May the God of peace . . . equip you with everything good for doing his will."

[2] 1 Timothy 6:10 (emphasis added).

[3] Matthew 6:24.

[4] Matthew 6:24.

[5] Acts 20:35.

[6] Mark 8:36.

[7] Genesis 22:1–18.

[8] Genesis 22:2.

[9] Luke 22:42: "Father, if you are willing, take this cup from me; yet not my will, but yours be done."

[10] Genesis 22:12.

[11] Matthew 5:41.

CHAPTER 3

Obedience

"A world of confusion results from trying to believe
without obeying."
—*A.W. Tozer*[1]

True Change or Not?

What is it that God wants from you? Does He
want you to go to church every week or twice a
week? Does He want your regular and consistent
tithes, offerings and sacrifices? Does He want you to
stop smoking, drinking and dancing? We could ask
many questions to try and discover exactly what God
wants from us. And in fact He may prefer that we
change many of the behaviors in our lives. But the
truth is that God wants only two things above all else
from each of us. First, He wants us to live our lives
trusting, believing and turning to Him through His
Son. Second, He wants us to be obedient to His
words and commandments.

"Okay" you say "but how do I make that happen in my life?" We can say we believe and want a heartfelt relationship with God but how do we actually do it? The answer is through obedience and by following examples that have been provided for us.

We all know what it is to obey someone. In our desire to become more obedient to the Lord what do we use as our guide or signposts? How do we know what our obedience looks like if we don't know God or His Word? What if we don't know what the scriptures (Bible, Torah, Koran, Vedic, Four Noble Truths, or Eight-Fold Path) say?

How are we to know what we are to do if we don't read or know these books of scriptural stories?

The Lord is well aware of how difficult and complicated we like to make our lives. He has been watching us do so since the first people walked the earth. Believe it or not His idea has always been to keep it very simple and easy for us to understand. God gave Moses Ten Commandments by which the followers of Judeo-Christian beliefs could know His guiding words. If He thought we needed more, He would have given us more. God knew that the words He gave Moses on the tablets for the Israelites would be enough to cover virtually every situation we could find or get ourselves into.

So if you are unfamiliar with the scriptures, if you aren't sure what God's Word is or says to you, if you don't read or have never read the Bible, all you need to remember is to live your daily life according to

God's ten guiding sentences of ethical and moral behavior; His Ten Commandments.[2] With a working knowledge of these ten you will always be ready to face any situation, conflict or choice, for in them God has given us His ways. Of the ten, four deal with your relationship with God and six pertain to your relationship with other people. Here they are:

• **Love God first and most:** Above everyone and everything else your relationship with God is paramount. We accomplish this by having a heart felt relationship with God through His Spirit and by knowing the thoughts, words, and deeds of His Son.

• **Keep God above all other wants, needs, or desires (other gods or idols):** As shared earlier, money and possessions have become the idolatries of our twenty-first century lives. In Old Testament times, idols might have been livestock or fertility statues. Today it's a new Lexus or BMW. If you put the things of your life in their proper order by placing God first in your heart, all of your other needs will be provided for.[3]

• **Never use the Lord's name in vain:** That is, never damn anything or anyone using God's name.[4]

• **Keep holy the Sabbath:** Whether your Sabbath

is Saturday, Sunday or some other time of the week, take time consistently and often for your relationship with God and His Son to grow and develop.[5]

These four are the "do's" of the Ten Commandments. You'll notice that these refer to your relation-ship with God. Now what about the others?

• **Honor your father and mother:** Honor is a form of respect. We should give honor to our own parents (and to our in-laws) just as we honor God the Father. Now you'll notice that God didn't use the word "love" in this commandment. He used "honor" because even if we are unable to love our parents for whatever reason, they still merit our respect for who they are in our lives and families.

• **Do not lie.**
• **Do not cheat.**
• **Do not steal.**
• **Do not murder.**
• **Do not covet (envy).**

The last five are pretty self explanatory and they are the "don'ts." You'll notice that these last six commandments pertain to our relationships with each other.

There you have it. Ten ways to lead you in all of your decisions, choices, actions and behaviors. If we would learn and apply them in our lives we would have all the guidelines we need for every situation we could possibly get ourselves into. Think about it for a minute. Try to come up with one situation in your life where one of these would not apply.

"What if I can't remember all ten?" you may ask. The Lord has already thought of this for you. If for some reason you have difficulty remembering all ten or in the heat of the moment you can't remember which one may apply to a situation you find yourself in, you need know only two.

First, "Love the Lord your God with all your heart and with all your soul and with all your mind." And second, "Love your neighbor as yourself."[6] Or as you may know it in its modern vernacular "the Golden Rule": "Do unto others as you would have them do unto you." If you can know, remember and practice these two in all your encounters, you will learn much, have peace and be blessed. By being obedient to at least these two, you will know the basic ways of God.

Now what about some examples? We use examples as the kingpins of our learning process from our earliest days as children. We learn the behaviors and actions of our world by watching and imitating others. We look to our parents, siblings, friends, heroes and finally our world, but where do we go to learn the essentials of the spirit? Where can we go to learn the way to a relationship with God if we don't go to church or if we have fallen away from our previous exposures to religious teachings? You can go to and with your spirit.

Remember we said that we were all born with a conscience, which is the essence of God living within us and thereby inherently know right from wrong.

It is through your mind that your conscience speaks to your thoughts but it is through your emotions that your conscience speaks to your heart. This is why the emotional pain of heartbreak is so much more intense than rationalization the wrongs which may have been done to you.

When you find yourself in a sticky situation and a decision or choice must be made, ask yourself "What should I do?" Then weigh the answer you get from your head with the emotional angst you feel in your heart. As a believer if you go with your heart you will be responding to the Lord.[7] This is easier to do if you are living and practicing truth in your life, but the fact of the matter is, most of us are not.

So how do we make the journey to that place? By having examples to follow and then by following them.

We already have enough worldly experiences and examples to follow but where do we as Christains find examples of truth? We look to the one who gives us living examples of the truth and of what God is really like. We look to the one God has provided for us as a living example of an obedient life, His Son Jesus.[8] By looking to Jesus we get a small glimpse of who God is and what He is really like.[9] Jesus came to be our example of God's way and how to change our lives if we choose to do so.

One of the reasons Jesus lived was to show us by example what God would have us do in each and every situation, for Jesus lived as we live. The same things that tempt us, tempted Him. He faced the same words, feelings and hatred that we experience. He came to show us that life could be lived truthfully and lovingly. By listening to His words, by understanding His thoughts and by emulating His behaviors we are able to become more Christ-like in our own lives. In this way we also become brothers and sisters to each other and to the Lord, which can only bring us closer to being people of God.[10]

What if you have never read any of His sayings or teachings? What if you don't know what Jesus' thoughts, words and deeds were? What if you have tried and you just couldn't get through all the "thees" and "thous" of the Bible stories, parables and scriptures? How do we find and follow the Word of God?

WWJD? Remember this acronym from a few years back that represented "What Would Jesus Do?"

The Christian community, especially its youth were caught up in the WWJD trend. For a brief moment in our time this ultimate question of behavioral response for ourselves and toward each other surfaced and had its "fifteen minutes of fame."

What happened to the promotion, the hype, the fad? It cycled as do all movements but the depth of the meaning behind those letters lives on. Greater still are the true implications of these letters and what they represent.

Ask yourself once again "What would Jesus do?" When you find yourself in any situation where a decision or choice must be made and you are in conflict as to the best or correct response, ask yourself "In this situation, what would Jesus do?" Your conscience will answer you, Christ will answer you, God will answer you. Whether you are a believer or not, whether you are a practicing Christian or not and whether you have a spiritual or religious background or not, if you ask, God will answer.

However when you ask and He answers, will you listen? Will you heed the instructions He gives? What will you choose to do and which path will you choose to walk when your question has been asked and answered?

God in His infinite wisdom has made things very simple so that we might understand more easily. In all of our dilemmas He has given us two telling questions to ask that will give us the answers and the truth we struggle to find.

Whenever a problem arises within your life lessons ask yourself these two questions: "Which will I choose, God's way or my way?" And "What Would Jesus Do?"

By asking these two questions and by remembering God's Ten Commandments or at least the basic "Two Commandments" ("Love God first and most" and "Love your neighbor as yourself") you will be able to deal with any problem that may cross your path that demands your time and attention.

If you have felt that a relationship with the Lord

God is unattainable, simply know that He is waiting for you to choose. Decide now and begin to live and enjoy the difference of blessings in your life today and every day.

Don't believe it? Try it. Come to God through His Son and step by step you will change and so will your life.

Change

At this point we should make one thing very clear; not all people are interested in changing their lives. This is a fact. Many people are happy with their current situations just as they are. They are determined to live their lives on their own terms at any cost, come what may. These people will tell you that they are in total control of their own lives and in some cases in control of other people's lives as well. They don't need anyone in their lives. They believe it and oftentimes they want to prove it.

You may also know or be aware of many successful and powerful people in your own community or elsewhere. What you may not know is many of these people have a dynamic living personal relationship with God. People in all areas of life are walking with the Lord and He continually blesses them. By outward appearances it may look as though they excel at their craft, skill, career, talent or relationships strictly on their own merit and efforts or because they seem to "get all the breaks." Likewise many of these children of God may not broadcast their individual or family spiritual beliefs and practices.

Oftentimes we think that someone who is not religiously or spiritually active as not having a close personal relationship with the Lord. Because someone doesn't know or quote scriptures does not mean they are spiritually lacking. And by contrast someone who is always quoting or espousing scripture may not have a relationship with God at all.

Whether walking with God or not we each "reap what we sow."[11] You have surely heard and may have even used this scripture on occasion. It is these few words that describe all of our efforts and their outcomes. This idea of sowing and reaping applies to all people, believers and followers of God's Word, as well as those who are not. Many couplets in the Old Testament book of Proverbs describe the believer and non-believer who both sow and reap. If you have ever read any Bible stories or examined parts of the Bible, Torah or Old Testament Jewish history you will find a common thread. When the people of Israel were obedient to God they were blessed. When they strayed from the Lord or were disobedient to His Word they were on their own and quite often suffered gravely. Why should we believe that it would be any different for us today?

Here again the Lord gives us free will to choose. If we choose to do everything on our own and in our own way then we will surely reap what we sow. Metaphorically in today's vernacular, the non-believer might say "You win some, you lose some, and some get rained out." The non-believer is truly on his or her own.

For the believer and follower of God's Word however, there is a very important connection that also underlies this concept. It is this single connection that takes our sowing and reaping to the next level for it is through this connection that our efforts are consistently blessed. It is our connection to the Lord as we plant and harvest within our lives. One of the truly magnificent aspects of God's love for you is that He wants to be right there with you as you sow your seeds and reap your harvest blessings.

God is always true to His Word and will never let you down. Just as He has done for thousands of years for those who trusted in Him and His Word and just as He did for Jesus, He will do for you today as a believer and follower of His Word.

You may disagree and say that you have trusted in the Lord and He has let you down, that you sowed and sowed while you believed yet still failed to reap the rewards and benefits. There is however, an aspect of God's love that is so amazing even believers sometimes overlook it.

It is when we want something so badly and we sow seeds diligently as we work for the harvest and are then devastated by failure. Later we find out that what we wanted and worked so hard for really wasn't a blessing at all and the true blessing the Lord had for us was in our *not* reaping successfully at that moment or in that place. We find by not reaping what we had so diligently sown we miraculously averted a minor or major tragedy.

If we choose to do it our way, we will reap what we sow. If we choose to do it God's way we will reap blessings in many forms. God loves and blesses obedience gladly in the same way every parent does.

Why should we risk changing from rebellion to obedience? For blessings. Why should we risk trusting in and believing the Lord and His words and ways, as we sow and reap? For blessings.

Once more, God blesses obedience. He loves us all but He also loves blessing those who turn to Him and trust in His Word instead of continually insisting on doing everything their own way.

We now know the "why" of change; to become more obedient to the Lord's Word. By becoming more obedient to God we become more like His Son Jesus Christ who is our example. And by becoming more Christ-like in our obedience we become a new creation[12] with new strength.[13] We become better people.

The next question is "how?" How do we change to be more obedient to the Lord's will? In a word; Repentance. Now don't run away. To repent simply means to change. It means changing from old ways to new ways of doing things and turning your back on your old patterns, responses and behaviors to risk walking a new path. Let's look at what it truly means to repent and learn the steps needed to accomplish it.

It has been recorded that Jesus' first words after starting the ministerial part of His life were "Repent, for the kingdom of God is near."[14] Now this could be interpreted in at least two ways. First that Jesus, the human manifestation of the Spirit of God[15] was present and therefore near. Or second, that for each and every one of us the kingdom of God is near in the form of "the end" (at least our end). For no matter who we are or how long we may live, our end is indeed near. The key is not how near our end may or may not be, but how and when we change our lives through our thoughts, words and deeds along the path to that end.

More often than not forgiveness is a part of true repentance. This is why repentance (change) is also the last important step in the process of forgiveness. Forgiving and true repentance (real change) go hand in hand.

When we commit a transgression and ask for or require forgiveness we must take the necessary steps to be forgiven. The seven steps of forgiveness are: recognition, responsibility, regret, remorse, redress, repetition and repent.

Obviously nothing can happen until we are prepared to (1) *recognize* that we have offended in some way. Once recognized the process of our request to be forgiven may begin. Next we must (2) take *responsibility* for what we have done (3) feel *regret* (4) have *remorse* (5) formulate some form of *redress* (6) realize that *repetition* (of the act or offense) is out of the question and finally (7) *repent* (truly change our behavior by never repeating it again in the future).

The reason repenting is so important is that

repentance is the action step needed to be forgiven. To truly repent a person must actually change his or her behavior. Without repentance the other six steps are for naught. And without a change in behavior there can be no forgiveness.

Repentance is also a fundamental aspect in the act of baptism for a Christian. The action of repentance is why many baptisms are done publicly. Baptism is an outward expression of an inward desire and as it cleanses us of our past, it requires us to repent (truly change our impending future actions) to obtain forgiveness. Baptism represents our desire to recognize and submit to God's will in our lives. It is our wish and our will to repent of our past actions and sins. Only by being prepared to respond differently in future situations can our repentance have validity. Our repentance is proven or disproved by our future actions, by whether we turn away from or repeat them.

How will we know how to respond in the future? Remember our question: "What would Jesus do?" Only by actually changing our responses, behaviors and actions in the future can our repentance be validated in the present and forgiveness granted for our actions of the past. In other words if one commits a transgression, confesses and asks for forgiveness and then subsequently repeats the offense or action again, it negates the act of forgiveness. In such a case the person repents but does not actually change his or her actions, responses and behaviors when confronted with the same temptation, test or situation again.

When the behavior hasn't changed, the person hasn't changed. The process has been an exercise in futility. The process of forgiveness is a "heart thing" with God, not a ceremony or rite that one goes through for the appearance or the approval of others.

One of the truly magnanimous aspects of God's love is that He is always willing to accept us with open arms and take us back again waiting for us to truly and finally answer His call.[16] Each time we try and fail and then call to Him once more, He answers and continues to wait for us to be repent and *truly change* our behavior. This is the commitment and the action of the repentant believer.

God never gets tired of us. He never tires of our efforts. He waits for us to start being obedient to His Word. When we are truly repentant and finally obedient, He is ready to forgive. And with obedience come the blessings that He promises to us.

Change your heart and your actions. Become obedient and be blessed. The choice as always is yours.

Endnotes

[1]
A. W. Tozer, "Our Wills Must Surrender," *Renewed Day by Day,* devotion dated June 20, compiled by Gerald B. Smith (Camp Hill, Pa.: Christian Publications Inc., 1991).

[2]
Exodus 20:3–17.

[3]
Matthew 6:8: "For your Father knows what you need before you ask him."

[4]
Luke 12:10: "Anyone who blasphemes against the Holy Spirit will not be forgiven."

[5]
Matthew 6:6: "When you pray, go into your room, close the door and pray to your Father, who is unseen."

[6]
Matthew 22:37, 39.

[7]
Acts 15:8: "God, who knows the heart . . . by giving the Holy Spirit . . . to us."

[8]
John 8:42: "For I came from God and now am here. I have not come on my own; but he sent me."

[9]
John 8:19: "If you knew me, you would know my Father also."

[10]
1 John 4:16: "God is love."

[11]
Galatians 6:7.

[12]
2 Corinthians 5:17: "If anyone is in Christ, he is a new creation; the old is gone, the new has come!"

[13]
1 Corinthians 10:13: "No temptation has seized you except what is common to man. And God is faithful: he will not let you be tempted beyond what you can bear. But when you are tempted, he will also provide a way out so you can stand up under it."

[14] Mark 1:15: "The time has come. . . . Repent and believe the good news!"

[15] John 3:16: "For God so loved the world that he gave his one and only Son."

[16] Luke 11:10: "For everyone who asks receives; he who seeks finds; and to him who knocks, the door will be opened."

CHAPTER 4

Faith
(Understanding, Prayer, Petition, Patience)

Understanding

The common thread that ties all aspects of our spiritual life together is faith. When we are finally willing to surrender our possessions as the motivators of our hearts we discover something important about our lives and ourselves. The world wants us to have faith in ourselves. It shows us through trial and error that in many cases we can trust and have faith only in ourselves and even that can be on shaky ground. We also find that we are tested often more intensely than ever before. When we seek to find and dwell with the Lord in our hearts we begin to live free as never before. In our obedience to the God's Word we find that our "tests" become nothing more than "pop-quizzes."

We ask "What is faith?" We are asked "Do you have faith?" Of course our answer is yes but how can we describe our faith? Who and what do we adhere to? Ourselves again? If we don't have faith how do we acquire it?

One of the best and most succinct definitions of faith comes from the book of Hebrews in the New Testament. Chapter 11 verse 1 reads "Faith is being sure of what we hope for and certain of what we do not see."

At the center of the Christian experience of faith is a belief in the invisible and a focus on an unseen reality; God.

Many believe that God is, but is what? Is His name a label we use to describe concepts like goodness, truth, love or a great unseen energy? Some identify God as the spark behind the phenomenon of life. For some God is only a philosophical inference. Many more believe as Conan Holmes of India noted "He must be, at least we think that He is." This proclamation rings true for many today who make it without much conviction or in an almost questioning manner.

The French author and philosopher Voltaire once wrote "If God did not exist, it would be necessary to invent Him."[1] Many claim that He exists but certainly not as a personality. Others know of God only by hearsay and some don't know Him at all. Each of these ideas about God has one thing in common; He is unknown to the individual as a personal reality. Even many "Christians" go through life trying to be loyal to principles and creeds or to love a concept or ideal. God is no more a personal being for them than He is to the non-Christian or the non-believer.

We know and believe in the physical world as being real for we know it through our five senses. And we certainly have no trouble believing in the spiritual world of the devil, demons and evil forces but we continue to deny the existence of God and His Son with a similar veracity. Our selfishness and sinful nature have clouded our hearts so that we fail to see the light of the Lord shining visibly all around us. Faith as described in the above passage from Hebrews 11 is rooted in our ability to believe. As believers we possess the faculties needed to see, if only we would obey the Spirit's urging of us to use them and personally come to know God and His Word.

It is through the attachments of our physical senses to the things of the world that the world triumphs. Ever since Adam hid in disgrace from God in the Garden of Eden and blamed his disobedience on Eve, mankind has steadily become more and more separated and distant from the great unseen reality that is God.

A story in the book of Numbers from the Old Testament shows us an example of faith in action. "Then the Lord sent venomous snakes among them; they bit the people and many Israelites died. The people came to Moses and said "We sinned when we spoke against the Lord and against you. Pray that the Lord will take the snakes away from us." So Moses prayed for the people. The Lord said to Moses "Make a snake and put it up on a pole; anyone who is bitten can look at it and live."

So Moses made a bronze snake and put it up on a pole. Then when anyone was bitten by a snake and looked at the bronze snake, he lived."[2]

Jesus shared this same story that we might better understand this important concept of faith and a relationship with God. Jesus explained how we might be saved. He told His listeners (and us) that it is by believing: "Just as Moses lifted up the [bronze] snake in the desert, so the Son of Man must be lifted up, that everyone who believes in him may [be saved and] have eternal life."[3]

Perhaps you saw the 1994 motion picture *The Santa Clause* starring Tim Allen. In one scene Eric Lloyd who played the son tells Tim Allen, "For adults seeing is believing but for kids 'believing is seeing.'"

Believing is Seeing

For the Christian, believing is seeing. It can be done any time and any place. You are no nearer to God on Christmas Day or Easter Sunday than on Wednesday June 23 or Friday November 6. In this same way believing can be done without any specific religious training, background, equipment or paraphernalia. For true followers of God and His Word believing *is* seeing.

This is why Jesus admonishes His listeners in Mark 10:15 "Anyone who will not receive the kingdom of God like a little child will never enter it." One must come to God with the purity and innocence of heart that is found in a child or a new, born-again believer. It is this kind of belief that will open your heart so that the invisible will become seen and known. God can be seen from anywhere and at any time if your mind and heart are set to believe, love and obey Him. Lift your eyes to God and rest your heart and mind upon Him. Immediately you will be at peace, for God works from the inside out. Now when we are asked the question what is faith? We may answer assuredly "faith is the gaze of my soul upon God."[4]

As we practice our faith, it becomes more than an isolated thought; it becomes part of our growing relationship with God as we begin to do the work of God. As Jesus explains about faith in response to those who ask about coming to God through works "The work of God is this; to believe in the one he has sent."[5]

Prayer and Petition

If faith is our connection to establishing a living relationship with the Lord yet we do not spend time with Him or have a biblical or spiritual background that allows us to feel comfortable with God's words, what are we to do? How are we to approach God if our feelings of inadequacy leave us lost and wondering?

Once again, God has provided us with a simple answer; "Do not be anxious about anything but in everything by prayer and petition with thanksgiving, present your requests to God."[6] "Great idea" you respond "but I don't know what to say or even how to ask."

When Jesus was teaching the people of His own day who were feeling separated and isolated from God through spiritual ignorance or lack of exposure and education He instructed them in His Sermon on the Mount about prayer.

Very few people have not heard of the Lord's Prayer. In these few sentences Jesus brings the kingdom of God; past, present and future into our very lives on a daily basis or whenever we want, need or desire. If we know nothing else about or from the Bible, this prayer alone is enough for us to make our connection with God every time we take a minute to pray and commune with Him.

For those who may not be familiar with this prayer we will take a moment to examine and see its value as our conduit to and with God. (There may be minor variations in the actual wording used from one presentation to another and from one translation and/or edition to others. Therefore, what is shown here may be slightly different than what you may know, read or use.)

Our Father in heaven, hallowed be your name,
your kingdom come, your will be done on earth as it is
in heaven.
Give us today our daily bread.
Forgive us our debts as we also have forgiven our
debtors.
And lead us not into temptation, but deliver us from
the evil one
[for yours is the kingdom and the power and the glory
forever].[7]
Amen.

When our Lord Jesus spoke to the many people gathered to hear Him, He spoke to a collective audience. For the moment however, we will look at the Lord's Prayer in a more personal way than you may have in the past. As we examine it in depth I invite you to make it more personal. For this reason and for our study, I have rewritten it here as follows:

Our Father who is in heaven, holy be your name.
Your kingdom come, your will be done in my life on
earth as it is in heaven.
Give me this day my daily bread.
Forgive me my trespasses as I forgive those who
trespass against me.
Lead me out of temptation, and deliver me from the
evil one,
for yours is the kingdom and the power and the glory
forever.
Amen.

Notice that Jesus begins with "our Father" not just His Father but *our* Father, meaning that the Lord God is the Father of *all of us* and of all things.[8]

He then continues with "who is in heaven," telling us (1) that God does exist and (2) where He may be found.[9]

"Holy [sacred] be your name" God is deserving and worthy of our respect, our worship and our praise. He is holy, thereby defining holiness and its essence.[10]

"Your kingdom come" the kingdom of God (heaven) is in fact to be and will exist.[11] Through these words His kingdom is here for us today.

"Your will be done in my life" it is God's will in our lives, now and in the future that should be paramount to our understanding of our actions and their consequences.[12]

"On earth as it is in heaven" explains that God's will is to be obeyed in our lives here in this reality on earth just as it is adhered to in heaven.[13]

"Give me this day my daily bread" we are to pray for and recognize every day both our mortal and spiritual sustenance.[14]

"Forgive me my trespasses [debts] as I forgive those who trespass against me [my debtors]" if we are to be forgiven for our sins and inequities we must be ready, willing and able to forgive those who have wronged us.[15]

"Lead me out of temptation" the Lord cannot and would not lead us into temptation. We are able enough to do that for ourselves. In fact He attempts to lead us out of temptation every time we stray. Remember that we can have only one thought at a time and it is the temptation of our thoughts that lead us into sin. Be assured that when the world gives us temptations and burdens to test us, God always gives us a way to cope at that moment and a way out of our sinful actions.[16]

"And deliver me from the evil one" it is through Christ our Savior that God has provided for our deliverance and redemption from Satan, sin and death itself.[17]

"For yours is the kingdom and the power and the glory forever, Amen." Everything is God's and only He has the power to make it so. It is to Him that we as believers both in heaven and earth, should and must give all honor and glory.[18]

So the next time you talk with God and use the Lord's Prayer, why not make it personal and make it your own? Take a moment to speak it slowly that you might be able to listen to the words again and dwell upon their meaning for you in your daily life.

Patience

God has a plan for your life. In fact God has a plan for everyone's life.[19] God's plan is for you to come to know Him and then to know Him again through His Son, Jesus.

This is exciting news. As we saw before in our cycle scenarios in Chapter 1, nothing is more uplifting for the new believer than finally turning to God with a new heartfelt devotion. We may soon realize however that this experience might turn out to be more disappointing and much less invigorating than we originally thought. Why is this? And why does our bubble burst? In a word; timing.

God's timetable is much different than ours.[20] One of the great paradoxes of this life is that there seems to be enough time for everything until we realize there isn't and there seems to be little need for patience but the need for it is great.

The path that leads to the Lord requires patience. The experience of a living relationship with the Lord is built upon our patiently waiting on His guidance. Patience is part and parcel of our faith for they go hand in hand. As believers of God's Word and followers of His Son, faith is the foundation of our attitude, belief and perception but patience is both our keel and rudder giving balance and direction to our actions.

Patience is the one virtue we have very little of and the one we need most to see the wonders and workings of the Lord in our lives, for it is through patience that the blessings of obedience are revealed.[21]

Remember "It's the journey, not the destination."

Endnotes

1 Francois Marie Arouet (1694–1778).

2 Numbers 21:6–9.

3 John 3:14–15.

4 A. W. Tozer, *The Pursuit of God,* The Tozer Library (Camp Hill, Pa.: Christian Publications Inc., 1999), chapter 7.

5 John 6:29.

6 Philippians 4:6.

7 Matthew 6:9–13 [including footnote].

8 1 Corinthians 8:6: "Yet for us there is but one God, the Father, from whom all things came and for whom we live."

9 Matthew 7:21: "My Father who is in heaven."

10 Leviticus 11:45: "Because I am holy."

11 Matthew 25:34: "Come, you who are blessed by my Father; take your inheritance, the kingdom prepared for you since the creation of the world."

12 Ephesians 5:17: "Therefore do not be foolish, but understand what the Lord's will is."

13 Hebrews 12:10: "But God disciplines us for our good that we may share in His holiness."

14 John 6:35: "Then Jesus declared, 'I am the bread of life.'"

15 Matthew 6:14: "For if you forgive men when they sin against you, your heavenly Father will also forgive you."

[16] James 1:13–14: "When tempted, no one should say, 'God is tempting me.' For God cannot be tempted by evil, nor does He tempt anyone; but each is tempted when, by his own evil desire, he is dragged away and enticed."

[17] Psalm 3:8: "From the Lord comes deliverance."

[18] 1 Samuel 2:8: "For the foundations of the earth are the Lord's; upon them he has set the world."

[19] Jeremiah 29:11–13: "'For I know the plans I have for you,' declares the Lord, 'plans to prosper you and not to harm you, plans to give you hope and a future. Then you will call upon me and come and pray to me, and I will listen to you. You will seek me and find me when you seek me with all your heart.'"

[20] 2 Peter 3:8: "With the Lord a day is like a thousand years, and a thousand years are like a day."

[21] Malachi 3:7, 10: "'Return to me, and I will return to you,' says the Lord Almighty. . . . 'Test me in this,' says the Lord Almighty, 'and see if I will not throw open the floodgates of heaven and pour out so much blessing that you will not have room enough for it.'"

Part 2
Belief

"Believe that life is worth living and your belief will
help create the fact."
—*William James, 1842–1910*

CHAPTER 5

Christianity (and Other World Religions)

Many different religions and spiritual belief systems are practiced in the world today. Many have hundreds or even thousands of years of historical foundation and traditions. Some have spurred tangential offshoots of belief and practice. A few have incorporated the tenets of one or more to serve a purpose of greater understanding of the immense breadth and depth of God and His love and power.

To better understand the world's major belief systems and to have an opportunity to compare and contrast their fundamentals, we will be looking at seven major religious and spiritual belief systems. We will pose the same nine questions for each after a short descriptive overview paragraph.

The general descriptions, questions, and answers presented here for the seven major religious belief systems are reprinted with permission from an article published in print and on the Internet by the Elizabeth Church of Christ in Elizabeth, Australia.

The questions are:

1. How did we get here?
2. What is the purpose of life?
3. Who/what is God?
4. Who are humans?
5. What is sin?
6. How do you explain pain and suffering?
7. Has God communicated with us? How?
8. How do you find God?
9. What happens when you die?

Christianity

The word "Christianity" is taken from the name of Jesus Christ's followers: Christians. In other words, Christianity is for people who believe that Jesus, is the Son of God, is the only way to find the eternal God and is God manifested in the flesh. Below are some of the fundamentals of Christianity.

How Did We Get Here?

God created the universe, this world and everything on it in six days. On the sixth day He created humans. He could have created everything in a split second and He could have taken six trillion years but He chose to do it in six days. Animal species did not evolve from lower life forms but were all created separately to show God's incredible creativity. After He created humans He noted that all of creation was "very good."

What is the Purpose of Life?

Life finds meaning and purpose in a fulfilled relationship with God, the one who created us. To the extent that we're not in a fulfilled relationship with God, our lives lose purpose and focus. God did not create humans because He *needed* to. He created them because He *wanted* to. He wants us to know Him and knowing Him means much more than knowing *about* Him. It means an increasing trust relationship built over time that can weather any storm.

Who/What is God?

God is three persons in one being, often called the Trinity. Christians don't make up information about God; they find out what He is like from the pages of the Bible. The three persons who are each God, but are distinct from each other are God the Father, God the Son (Jesus), and God the Holy Spirit. No one has ever seen God the Father or God the Holy Spirit but many people saw God the Son while Jesus lived on earth in the Middle East.

The Bible tells us that if we want to see what God is like, we'll find out by looking at what Jesus is like. Here are a few character traits of Jesus: He
  • is compassionate toward people
  • forgives people of their sin

- is angry at hypocrisy and injustice
- has power to control the elements of nature
- is genuinely concerned with "outsiders"
- is concerned about every person individually
- leads by serving others
- is the only way to find God.

Who Are Humans?

Human beings are unique creations of God. No one is ever an accident in God's eyes. Everyone is born with the potential to live either a productive or a destructive life. This is why we see the likes of Adolf Hitler and the Mother Teresa. Most people are not at these extremes and struggle by varying degrees with desires to do good as well as evil. Men and women are fearfully and wonderfully made by God and are *not* the accidental byproduct of evolutionary chance. Every person has the opportunity to have a relationship with God.

What is Sin?

Sin, at its core is the pride of believing we don't need God. Pretty much every individual sin we could think of stems from this. Humans are born with an inclination to sin, which separates us from God. Sin is the one and only thing that keeps us from having a relationship with God. As soon as sin is dealt with in a person's life that person is free from the power of sin and is able to fully enjoy life.

How Do You Explain Pain and Suffering?

Pain and suffering are the result of sin being present in this world. Put simply, if there were no sin there would be no pain and no suffering. God is not the cause of suffering but nothing takes place that God doesn't know about. One writer said that pain was God's megaphone to a deaf world. In other words, pain wasn't part of the plan but God will use it to get through to people who otherwise would not be interested in Him.

Has God Communicated with Us? How?

Yes. God has communicated with us through His Word, the Bible. The Bible contains the Old and New Testaments. The word "testament" simply means "covenant" or "agreement." The Old Testament records the history of creation up until the time that Jesus lived on earth. God spoke through prophets in the Old Testament and their words are recorded there. The New Testament records the time Jesus was on earth until about thirty years after He left. Both testaments make up the Bible. God has revealed an incredible amount of detail about Himself throughout the pages of the Bible. Ultimately the best communication we have from God is Jesus. Jesus is God's revelation to us.

How Do You Find God?

You search for Him. God has promised that if people search for Him they will find Him. God isn't in the business of playing hard-to-get. In fact God has made it incredibly simple to find Him. There is only one way to God. This takes away the uncertainty of wondering which road will lead to God. The one way to find God is Jesus. When a person finds Jesus, he or she has found God.

What Happens When You Die?

Here's what does *not* happen when a person dies: he or she is not reincarnated, is not annihilated and does not automatically go to heaven. What happens at death depends on one thing only: whether the individual was in a relationship with God. Anyone who is in a relationship with God through the free gift of Jesus goes to be with God at the moment of death. This is a place of no more pain, suffering, regret, remorse or guilt. Those who are not in a relationship with God have effectively chosen their own destiny. Since they are not interested in a relationship with God on earth, God allows them to continue to be apart from Him for the rest of eternity. The Bible calls this hell. Many unwarranted descriptions of hell have been built up over the years. While hell and heaven are for eternity, hell is primarily regret and remorse at missed opportunities and the fact that there are no more "second chances." For those who trust in nothing but what Jesus has done for them on the cross, death and the afterlife hold no fear.

Judaism

The word "Judaism," as with the word "Jew,"

comes from one of the pre-eminent tribes of the nation of Israel, "Judah." The nation of Israel is not simply geographical; it is also political and religious. The word "Israel" means "he struggles with God." In other words, Judaism is for people who believe that the one true God is Yahweh, revealed in the Old Testament writings. Judaism differs from Christianity mainly because Jews are still waiting for a promised Messiah (the anointed one) whereas Christians believe that Jesus of Nazareth was that promised Messiah. Below are some of the fundamentals of Judaism.

How Did We Get Here?

God created the universe and everything on the earth within six days. God created Adam and Eve on the sixth day. He pronounced His creation "very good."

What is the Purpose of Life?

The purpose of life is to act responsibly toward God, the community, to oneself and to make good ethical choices. Tied in with this are the responsibilities to pass the traditions and celebrations of Judaism down through the generations.

Who/What is God?

There is one true God, revealed as the eternal "I am." In fact, devout Jews will neither say the name Yahweh nor write it in full. One of the best descriptions of God is found in the book of Psalms:

Yahweh is compassionate and gracious, slow to anger and abounding in love. He will not always accuse, nor will He harbor His anger forever. He does not treat us as our sins deserve or repay us according to our iniquities.[1]

Who Are Humans?

Each person is an individual, a special creation of God, fearfully and wonderfully made by Him. Humans are to live in the world God created, exercise free will and cooperate with God's guidance.

What is Sin?

In Judaism, sin is not following the teachings, precepts and laws set down in the Old Testament and particularly the Torah. The Torah is the collection of the first five books: Genesis, Exodus, Leviticus, Numbers and Deuteronomy. Various groups within Judaism incorporated new laws in an attempt to completely regulate the conduct of people. These extra laws are not part of the Old Testament. God is primarily looking for people whose hearts are seeking after Him.

How Do You Explain Pain and Suffering?

Ever since the sin of Adam and Eve all humans have had a tendency toward evil as well as toward good. Evil results from the choice to do wrong and to satisfy personal needs ahead of the needs of others. It is unknown why God allows the innocent to suffer but some Jews believe that suffering results from sins earlier in life. The focus is on knowing that God will punish those who do evil.

Has God Communicated with Us? How?

God has communicated with humans through the prophets and others who contributed to the Old Testament. All that is needed for life is found in this series of books.

How Do You Find God?

You find God by seeking Him. God has promised in the Old Testament that if anyone truly searches for Him, He will let Himself be found by that person.

What Happens When You Die?

There is very little said in Judaism about the afterlife. The concept is vague as the focus is far more on this life. Jews are looking for a time when the promised Messiah will come to usher in an age of paradise. They believe that even if they die, they will be raised again when paradise arrives.

Islam

The word "Islam" means "submission." A Muslim is one who submits. The submission is to be done to Allah, which literally means "the God." The word "Islam" is related to the word for peace. In other words Islam is for people, who believe that they must submit to Allah and that in doing so will find true peace. Below are some of the fundamentals of Islam.

How Did We Get Here?

We were created by Allah.

What is the Purpose of Life?

The purpose of life is to make a moral order in the world. This is also the goal of Islam.

Who/What is God?

Part of a Muslim's daily practice is to recite the creed "There is no God but Allah, and Mohammed is His prophet." This shows clearly that Muslims believe in one God. They reject the notions of many gods (Hinduism, Animism) and the Trinity (Christianity). They do not believe that Jesus is God, as Christians do, but do believe that Jesus was one in a line of prophets. Mohammed is the last and greatest prophet. Allah is portrayed as having majesty and might and His most important feature is justice. While these aspects are similar to the God of the Bible, Allah does not show grace, mercy, love or patience.

Who Are Humans?

Humans are created by Allah and are meant to be in charge of the creation under the authority of Allah.

What is Sin?

Sins are generally the evil things done by humans. Infidels are not tolerated in Islam. On the final great Day of Judgment all those who are not Muslims will find themselves in hell, which is described in the Quran (also spelled Koran) as a place of torment. Muslims disagree as to whether these torments should be taken literally or not.

How Do You Explain Pain and Suffering?

Islam teaches that humans are not inherently sinners but have been given free will to choose good or evil. This includes belief or unbelief in Allah and the consequences. Islam teaches that Satan and his spirits inhabit the earth and rule over non-believers. This accounts for evil and suffering. Nevertheless suffering is allowed by Allah to erase a person's sins and to test that person's humility and faith.

Has God Communicated with Us? How?

Allah has communicated with humans by giving the Quran to the great prophet Mohammed. The Quran contains what is needed to live life in the right way.

How Do You Find God?

Humans find Allah by accepting the guidance offered in the Quran.

What Happens When You Die?

People who are saved will experience the bliss of heaven, while those who are not saved will experience the torture of hell. On Judgment Day, Allah will resurrect the dead, unite bodies and souls and judge all for eternity in heaven or hell.

Buddhism

"Buddhism" is a word used to denote the teachings of the "Buddha" or "enlightened one." Guatama Buddha lived in the sixth century B.C.E. and set forth the teaching called the Middle Way, a path to escape suffering. This was a path in life between extreme asceticism and luxury. In other words Buddhism is for people who believe that Guatama Buddha discovered the true way to escape pain and suffering. Below are some of the fundamentals of Buddhism.

How Did We Get Here?

The cosmos has no known beginning or end. Rather it goes through cycles. We found ourselves on this earth through a process of cause and effect.

What is the Purpose of Life?

The purpose of life, put simply is to escape suffering and reach Nirvana. Nirvana literally means "blowing out" and can be vaguely understood as a permanent state of nothingness. Nirvana can be reached only after a person has escaped from continual reincarnation by following the Noble Eightfold Path:

1. Right belief
2. Right attitude
3. Right speech
4. Right bodily action
5. Right livelihood

6. Right effort
7. Right self-awareness
8. Right meditation

Once a person has escaped the cycle of reincarnation he has escaped suffering and has reached Nirvana. The purpose of his existence is fulfilled.

Who/What is God?

Contrary to popular understanding there is no god in the teachings of Buddhism. Guatama Buddha never claimed to be god nor did he claim to have any special revelation from a god.

Who Are Humans?

According to the teachings of Buddha, humans as with all creatures are fictions; they are non-existent. A person has no "self" and so the word "myself" has no meaning. Instead humans are a series of cause and effect occurrences that only *appear* to be complete persons.

What is Sin?

Sin in Buddhism is the belief that the world and the self truly exist. According to Buddhism they do not exist. This ignorance keeps the eternal cycle of suffering and the cosmos moving.

How Do You Explain Pain and Suffering?

Pain and suffering are the result of believing that the world and the self exist. In particular they result from craving for things. The only way to escape suffering is to recognize the Four Noble Truths and to follow the Eightfold Path. The Four Noble Truths are as follows:

1. Life is suffering
2. That suffering comes from craving for things
3. The suffering will stop when the craving stops
4. The way to stop craving is to follow the Noble Eightfold Path

Has God Communicated with Us? How?

No. There is no god to communicate.

How Do You Find God?

Again this question has no meaning. There is no god to find.

What Happens When You Die?

You will be reincarnated as a creature not necessarily in a better state than at present. Then you will eventually die again. Then you will be reincarnated and will die again. This will continue for an unknown time until, if possible, you reach Nirvana.

Hinduism

Hinduism is not so much a religion as a way of living. It began around the fourth century B.C.E. when the Aryans conquered India and brought their vast system of gods with them. The combination of the gods and the Indian tradition of meditation combined to form what is now known as Hinduism. In other words Hinduism is for people who believe that life is all about escaping the endless cycles of rein-carnation and ultimately becoming one with the ultimate consciousness, Brahman. Below are some of the fundamentals of Hinduism.

How Did We Get Here?
According to Hinduism the universe has no beginning and no end. In fact the universe is only an illusion since the one true reality is Brahman. Humans were not created. Instead each human soul, like the universe, has no beginning and no end. The human soul has always been here and goes through cycles of reincarnation and rebirth.

What is the Purpose of Life?
The purpose of life is to do more good things than bad things. In this way your next life will be in a better state than this one. This is the concept of "karma."

Who/What is God?
Hindus vary in their beliefs about god. Some believe there are no gods. Others believe there are at least thirty-three million gods. Usually Brahman is seen as the supreme god. However he is an impersonal being, completely above and uninvolved with the material universe (which is only an illusion anyway). Brahman is the one ultimate reality. The

other two powerful gods are Shiva and Vishnu. Shiva represents both the creative and destructive sides of godhood. Vishnu has shown himself many times through history. These include appearances as Rama, a good king and Krishna, an impetuous, violent, and erotic figure.

Who Are Humans?

Humans, like every other aspect of the universe, are illusions.

What is Sin?

Sin in Hinduism is doing more bad things in life than good things. The penalty for this sin is to be reincarnated in a worse condition in the next life.

How Do You Explain Pain and Suffering?

Pain and suffering are the results of things done in previous lives. Thus all present suffering is completely deserved. This is the reason why the caste system in India has flourished so well. There is no reason to address the poverty and pain of the "untouchable" caste, since this poverty is the fault of those in this caste. Hinduism also teaches that all evil in this life will be repaid in the next life.

Has God Communicated with Us? How?

Brahman has not communicated with humans. However some guidance is gained through the Hindu priesthood, the Vedic scriptures, the appearances of certain gods and by following one's spiritual "guru" as a guide.

How Do You Find God?

Finding God (or gods) is not the issue. The important thing is to be released from the endless cycles of reincarnation, finally dissolve all personality and become one with the ultimate consciousness, Brahman. This is achieved by practicing yoga, living according to the Vedic scriptures and following a spirit guide.

What Happens When You Die?

You will be reincarnated. The condition of your next life will depend on how you lived this life. Then you will eventually die again. Then you will be reincarnated and die again. This will be repeated for an unknown time until if possible, you lose all personality and become one with the impersonal consciousness.

Animism

The word "Animism" comes from the Latin word "animus" meaning *spirit*. Animism is a religion that believes all objects, natural phenomena and living beings have souls. In other words animism is for people who believe that spiritual beings and forces have power over human lives and that humans must find out which spirits are impacting them. Below are some of the fundamentals of Animism.

How Did We Get Here?

Some Animists believe that the universe had no beginning. Others believe that everything was created by the gods or even by a "high god" who is too distant to be concerned with the lives of humans.

What is the Purpose of Life?

For the Animist life finds its purpose in observing the tribal norms of behaviors as well as the taboos. The gods and the ancestors must be honored and sacrifices must be made to them. Initiation must be undertaken when appropriate.

Who/What is God?

There are many gods and spirits found in everything from nature, including trees, animals and heavenly bodies. Perhaps there is one higher god over all other gods that acts as a unifying force.

Who Are Humans?

Human beings are in some sense, children of the gods. Possibly they are descendants of their semi-divine primal parents.

What is Sin?

Sins are any offenses that disturb human relationships with the gods or spirits. When humans commit sin, retribution and anger from the gods are expected and accepted.

How Do You Explain Pain and Suffering?

Pain and suffering are normally the results of sin. That is the gods and spirits cause suffering to fall on a person or a community when someone in that community has done something against them. This will often be in the form of disastrous weather or failed crops.

Has God Communicated with Us? How?

The high god is too far away to communicate with humans. Even the lower gods do not communicate with humans. These gods have no concern, mercy or love for humans. Their ways are not stable and are normally defined by the current context. They could probably be said to communicate with humans only when they dole out punishments and calamities on a community.

How Do You Find God?

Searching for god or the gods is a futile exercise. The gods are everywhere and are not supposed to be searched for. The gods will find you.

What Happens When You Die?

Not much is known about the afterlife. Animists believe that when someone dies, he will join the ancestors in the next life. However there is little information about the next life and it is possibly as unpredictable as this life.

Atheism

The word "atheism" is derived from "a" meaning 'not' and "theos" meaning "god." In other words atheism is for people who believe there is no god of any kind. Below are some of the fundamentals of atheism.

How Did We Get Here?

Who knows? The best guess is probably that we somehow evolved from primitive life forms. But there's no explanation for how the primitive life forms got here. For no reason at all the world came into existence and eventually so did we. That's about all we can say.

What is the Purpose of Life?

There is no possible long-term purpose of life from atheism. Life came about by accident and so anything that happens is completely by accident. The best way to live out life as an atheist would be to "eat, drink and be merry." If any purpose were to come to the fore it would probably be to be strong enough to survive. This is based on the "survival of the fittest" part of the theory of evolution. All people are simply byproducts of a cosmic accident and so the most logical way to approach life is to look out for "number one" and preserve self at all costs. Not surprisingly this is basically the unwritten credo of modern society.

Who/What is God?

There is no such thing or person as God. The word "god" is an invention of our minds to help those who are weak.

Who Are Humans?

Human beings like every other life form in existence are accidental byproducts of evolution. We would like to believe that we are the most advanced stage of the evolutionary process. There is no reason for humans to exist and no reason for humans not to exist.

What is Sin?

The word "sin" is an invention of the human mind. It is not possible for "sin" or morals or the concepts of right and wrong to derive from a belief in atheism. In fact morals are in direct conflict with the atheistic advance of evolution. Here the strong survive and the weak are eliminated. Morals (helping the weak) and evolutionary survival (eliminating the weak) cannot exist together.

How Do You Explain Pain and Suffering?

Pain and suffering are part and parcel of evolution. There is no reason for or purpose in suffering and if you suffer it's just bad luck. Perhaps suffering could be viewed as nature's way of sorting the strong from the weak. If life forms make it through suffering, they must be strong and therefore they deserve to continue living.

Has God Communicated with Us? How?

No. There is no god. Obviously there is also no communication.

How Do You Find God?

This is a meaningless question.

What Happens When You Die?

Your body returns to the elements of nature. There is no such thing as a soul or spirit and so there is no such thing as an afterlife. When you die, that's it. The end. No reincarnation and no judgment or payback for wrongs committed while on earth.

Spiritual Christianity

Just as there are many different religions and spiritual belief systems practiced in the world, there are also many different sects or denominations within those major systems. For the purposes of this book we have added one additional spiritual belief. For more information about "Spiritual Christianity" beyond what is published here, please go to www.fellowship-of-believers.com, a website of available collected works pertaining to "Spiritual Christianity."

Spiritual Christianity is best described as a denomination of Christianity for we believe in Jesus the Christ and are followers of His life, examples and teachings. We also believe that the individual's spiritual relationship with God is one of paramount importance for it is this spiritual connection that gives purpose and guidance for the individual in his or her daily life and coexistence with others.

As a Christian denomination we believe, agree and hold to be true much of what is stated previously in the Christianity overview and questions. However Spiritual Christianity differs in a number of ways from other Christian denominational beliefs. We trust in and believe God's Word as presented in the Bible but we also recognize elemental possibilities such as intelligent design, evolution, reincarnation, death and hell to be part and parcel of God's many ways. We acknowledge beliefs by others as described in their own scriptural teachings according to their traditions and by their leadership to be valid for them as parochial believers.

At the core of each of the world's religions is a founding figure who has expository teaching for his followers. As the comparative difference between each system emerges, the nuances of significant distinctions begin to come out of the shadows and into the light of knowledge and acceptance for each master and his beliefs. For example, it is Mohammed and the Koran, Buddha and the Eight Fold Noble Path, Krishna and philosophy, Zoroaster and ethics.

It is here that the fundamental similarities of each and subsequently the difference between the others and Jesus becomes increasingly evident. In the teachings of all five masters described, an instructive way of living is revealed. Yet it is not Mohammed who changes the listener, it is the Koran's instructive presentation. It is not Buddha who is the deliverer, it is the Four Noble Truths which instruct. It is not Krishna or Zoroaster to whom people turn, it is to their instruction. The pinnacle of separation is this; as with the others, not only did Jesus of Nazareth instruct and expound his teaching message, unlike any others, He *lived* His message and He *was* His message. Not only did He proclaim the truth, He stated "I am the truth." Not only did He show the way, He declared "I am the way." Not only did He offer up life, He revealed "I am the resurrection and the life." Of these five masters only one claimed the authority of reconciliation, redemption and salvation from sin. Only Jesus assured the world "I am the Alpha and the Omega." The follower of Jesus has the opportunity of relating to and being with the Holy Trinity and the fullness of the Godhead in human bodily form through Jesus the Christ.

Spiritual Christianity is more than a devotion to instructive living. Spiritual Christianity recognizes the holiness of God in three separate entities: Father, Son, and Spirit. We believe that God the Father created the universe and all initial matter. We believe that God's Spirit became flesh in the person of Jesus of Nazareth, who as the Christ is our Lord, savior and redeemer and that God's Spirit abides within the believer in the form of conscience (whether baptized or not). We believe God's Word to be truth, which comes from His unconditional love.[1]

Below are some of the fundamentals of "Spiritual Christianity."

How Did We Get Here?

Humans came into being by a creative act of God in concert with His own processes and through His continuous spiritual presence. We believe that God created the universe, our world and the process of life according to His own timetable and methods. Whether initial creation took a moment ("Big Bang"), six days,[2] six thousand years[3] or six million years is not the important point of origination. We believe that evolution is part of God's life process and at whatever point He was ready; the breath of God filled the world with living, animated potentiality. As for man, God either took the ground of earth creating Adam and breathing life into him ("creationism"). Or, God selected a Cro-Magnon individual (Homo Sapiens species prior to modern man) and breathed into him the four essential differences of progressive species life (1. language 2. the powers of relationship observation 3. rational and reasoning analysis and understanding and 4. a soul connection to Himself) not present in species before, and *made* Adam (via 'intelligent design' as part of the evolutionary process). Whether creation or evolution (both being "God's way") Adam was the first man with a reciprocal spiritual link to God. God is therefore the creator of "creationism" and the 'missing link' of "scientific evolution."

What is the Purpose of Life?

Our purpose is to know that God is God and that He exists, that we might glorify Him and know Him forever[4] and then to know God again through His Son, Jesus the Christ.[5]

Who/What is God?

God is the holy creator of the universe and all that is in it. God's spiritual manifestation in the man Jesus gives us a glimpse of the character and nature of God the Father through the thoughts, words and deeds of Jesus [6] as well as through other masters and teachers.

Who Are Humans?

Humans are creations of God.[7] We were created by God to take stewardship[8] of this world and its creatures that we might live in peace and harmony with each other and with the natural physical things on earth.

What is Sin?

Sins are the actions and behaviors of disobedience to God's Word as found in the Ten Commandments.[9]

How Do You Explain Pain and Suffering?

Pain and suffering come by God's power, by accident and by the forces of evil through Satan. One of God's ultimate desires is that we be obedient believers of His words. It is through our disobedience, our refusal to surrender to God's will and our personal and selfish desires that we "reap what we sow." God often times uses His power to

orchestrate events in our lives, both positive and negative to get our attention and to turn us to Him.[10]
Secondly, other events take place by sheer accident. Last but not least, in a battle[11] with the Lord God (good vs. evil) for the eternal capture of each one's soul and spirit, the forces of evil in the world under the influence and possible direction of Satan can cause pain and suffering.[12]

Has God Communicated With Us? How?

Yes. God has communicated in a number of ways (audibly[13] visually[14] tactilely[15] and subconsciously through dreams and visions[16]) through a variety of different people throughout history.

How Do You Find God?

Ask, seek and knock.[17] God is found by looking for Him, by exercising free will to have and pursue a relationship with Him and by inviting Him to be part of your individual daily life.[18] This can and should be done in a number of ways: praying and meditating, reading and studying scripture, fellowship with other believers and worshiping and praising God.

What Happens When You Die?

The soul of the believer in Jesus Christ[19] is baptized by His heavenly and holy fire[20] and then enters a place in heaven with the souls of other Christian believers until the last day and final judgment.

On that day, the souls of the living and the dead in Christ will be raised up (resurrected).[21] All believers will be given new names and identities in Christ[22] and will be with God Almighty in a universal heaven forever.

God's love is so great that upon death, the soul of the non-believer also goes to a place in heaven to perhaps be given another opportunity to come to know Jesus as the Christ through reincarnation (in human form at some future date prior to the final Judgment Day). There may be many reincarnation opportunities for the individual until the final day.[23] On that final Judgment Day believers and non-believers alike (for all are sinners)[24] will face judgment by the Son.[25]

For the repentant believer heaven will be exactly that: a "heavenly" experience within God's universal paradise. Believers will understand the holy love, truth, compassion, mercy, grace, forgiveness and consciousness of God and thereby become "children of God." However for the unrepentant non-believer at judgment, there will be either death (eternal oblivion; absence from God) or Hell. A place for those who have committed heinous acts and crimes against others and those who have acquiesced and submitted to the acknowledgement and worship of the Antichrist will experience that which they perpetrated upon others or worse, as God decides.

We hope this provides you with an understanding of the foundation and fundamentals of "Spiritual Christianity" in comparison with other world religious and spiritual belief systems.

By the way, what do you believe?

Endnotes

1
 Psalm 103:8–10.

2
 Genesis 1:1–31.

3
 2 Peter 3:8: "With the Lord a day is like a thousand years."

4
 Genesis 17:1: "I am God Almighty."

5
 Mark 9:7: "This is my Son, whom I love. Listen to him!"

6
 John 8:19, 8:42: "If you knew me, you would know my Father also . . . for I came from God and now am here."

7
 Genesis 1:26: "Then God said, 'Let us make man in our image.'"

8
 Genesis 1:26: "And let them rule over . . . all the earth, and over all the creatures."

9
 Exodus 20:1–17.

10
 Proverbs 16:9: "In his heart a man plans his course, but the Lord determines his steps."

11
 Ephesians 6:12: "For our struggle is not against flesh and blood, but against . . .the spiritual forces of evil."

[12] Job 1:7: "Satan answered the Lord, 'From roaming through the earth and going back and forth in it.'"

[13] Genesis 17:1: "I am God Almighty."

[14] Exodus 3:4: "God called to him from within the bush."

[15] Exodus 32:16: "The tablets were the work of God; the writing was the writing of God, engraved on the tablets."

[16] Genesis 37:5: "Joseph had a dream."

[17] Matthew 7:7–8: "Ask and it will be given to you; seek and you will find; knock and the door will be opened to you."

[18] Revelation 22:17: "Whoever is thirsty, let him come; and whoever wishes, let him take the free gift of the water of life."

[19] John 11:26: "And whoever lives and believes in me will never die."

[20] Matthew 3:11: "He will baptize you with the Holy Spirit and with fire."

[21] John 11:25: "I am the resurrection and the life. He who believes in me will live, even though he dies; and whoever lives and believes in me will never die."

[22] Revelation 3:12: "And I will also write on him my new name."

[23] Matthew 24:36, 42: "No one knows about that day or hour. . . . Therefore keep watch, because you do not know on what day your Lord will come."

[24] 1 Kings 8:46: "For there is no one who does not sin."

[25] John 5:22: "Moreover, the Father judges no one, but has entrusted all judgment to the Son."

CHAPTER 6

The Wheel of Life

The most perfect shape is a circle, for it encounters the least resistance and exhibits the greatest balance. If you have ever had a wheel that is "out of round" you know that the ride may become a little bumpy or skewed.

Have you ever watched as your car or truck is fitted and aligned with new tires? If so you have probably noticed that the repairman often places a small lead weight at a particular place on the wheel rim. He does this to bring the wheel fitted with the new tire as close to perfect balance as possible. Just that small amount of additional adjustment in the weight placement can make all the difference in the spin and subsequent wear of the tire. Not only is your ride smoother but the tire may last longer.

Our lives often resemble the wheel rims of our vehicles. Most of today's wheels are solid single units, sometimes with holes or gaps in the visual façades of the chrome-plated plastic covers, but are usually spoke less. They always appear to be in pretty good shape; strong, resilient and durable, until we look closely. We often don't notice the nicks, dings, chips or bends that are actually there. These are the telltale signs of imbalance wear and tear, as well as use and abuse that can cause our steering to pull a little to one side or our tire tread to wear a bit unevenly. Our tires become more and more vulnerable as our mileage totals increase over time.

The same may be said of your "wheel of life." When you are balanced, your wheel is spinning correctly and you enjoy more of a smooth ride of experiences. However even as you appear to be happily cruising down the path of life there may be a number of old patterns of behaviors, fears and doubts; the "nicks" and "dings" that can cause problems, distress and oftentimes "flats" or worse.

Within our society and world today it is easy for us to overlook or to cover up our imperfections and foibles because we are able to mask them with all the trappings of our modern times. As long as our outward appearances are viewed as we attempt present them, we are on cruise control flying down the fast lane of life.

Within the advent of shiny new high-tech chrome reverse style rim wheels of our lives, something has been lost: spokes. Today the only wheels you ever see consistently with spokes are on bicycles and with the current movement in the world of cycling, an ever increasing high-technology of bicycles have solid rim wheels as well.

From the first mass manufactured wheels up to and including vehicles of the first half of the twentieth century, most wheels had spokes. The spokes gave a wheel its integrity and strength and connected the rim to the hub. If a wheel was "out of round" one or more of the spokes would be adjusted, repaired or replaced and in doing so the wheel would be brought back into alignment and balance. Everyone today needs a "wheel of life" with spokes instead of "uni-body" solid-state rims.

What exactly is your "wheel of life"? For a moment, think of your life as the outer rim of a wheel, with each of the facets of your life being a spoke. (We will put your tire on later.)

In your "wheel of life" there is a spoke for each of the areas of your being, for example; physical, mental, emotional, psychological, social, rational, cognizant, identity, conscious, subconscious, visionary, spiritual as well as others. As was true with your lessons of life, each of your "wheel of life" spokes is interrelated and dependent upon the others. When one of your spokes is broken, bent or loose, it can influence the performance of one or more of the others by its effect on the rim's integrity, strength and balance.

When you were born you were just a rim. As you grew and learned from your experiences you slowly added, developed and worked on your spokes. As you put each spoke into place it had a binding and reciprocal effect on each of the others. As you spend time developing each one you find yourself experiencing strengths and weaknesses in your other spokes. Ideally you attempt to achieve a balance among all of your spokes so that the perfect roundness of your wheel will ensure a smooth and comfortable journey. Of course this is virtually impossible given the attributes and variables of our world.

We continue to strive and look for this balance, strength and integrity in all that we do, believing that this will ensure our ride control. This motivation for control over our lives will guide and lead us to different philosophical, religious and spiritual belief systems and experiences as we try to find the perfect spoke to explain the void we may be feeling inside. Many people have wandered from one realm of belief to another looking for the one that best represents a place of peace and understanding. All but one of the great spiritual masters did and millions continue to emulate their journeys in similar fashions.

As you grow and experience the different aspects of your life you are always giving more or less attention to each of your spokes by adjusting, tweaking, fitting, building up and shaving down. Always looking for the best combination to enhance and produce the best performance. The essential difference between your "wheel" and your "lessons" is that the internal spokes of your wheel are the foundations for the applications of your external actions and behaviors in your lessons. This is one of the reasons you may often retreat back to places from your past (especially to those of "insecurity") when you face turmoil in the lessons of the present. If one of your "spokes" is out of alignment for any reason it may have an inordinate amount of influence on your balance, causing problems and stress in both your wheel and in the lessons of your life.

Often times what you experience most is a struggle between the attention necessary for each spoke and its application within your lessons. Trying to accomplish this on your own and in of own control guarantees you many opportunities not only to make yourself crazy, but it also assures you of a very rough ride along the path.

How can you adjust your spokes both consecutively and concurrently to each other while going through all of your lessons at the same time? How do you bring more balance to your wheel? Remember how you solved the problem of working your way up the Triangle of Life? (Turn your Triangle upside down, and go to God first.) Your efforts with your "wheel of life" are similar. Instead of spirituality being one of the spokes you try to balance, make your spirituality the "hub" of your wheel instead. As before with your lessons of life when you went directly to God, now make your spiritual focus the hub, to which all of your other spokes attach and interconnect. In this way you will always have the strength and integrity necessary for continual balance.

Your spirituality is the one constant in your life. It connects not only all of the variables you experience in the world and in this life; it is also the element that connects you to the past, present and future of the entire universe. Your spiritual soul is you; "ever living." You are not your body or mind independently. Your body and mind are your existing physical and conscious realities in this time and place. It is your spirituality that is truly your life's energy. Your spiritual soul is your essence, your core, your "nuclear reactor." It is your spirituality (or lack thereof) that innately fuels and runs your mind and body. Your spiritual soul is the true you. It is your being, your essence and more importantly, your inner connection with God and His Spirit now and forever.

When your faith, understanding and adoration are placed in a leading founder or "enlightened prophet" of a religion or belief system, that person often becomes the focus or the "hub" of the believer's wheel. This can be true of all religious practices, regardless of what they may be called, labeled or named. If the principles and practices of a faith were unabashedly the same today and their adherence the same as when they originated, then placing allegiance in its spiritual founder would be the ultimate exercise in fellowship and discipline.

The problem is that no religion can escape the fact that its principles and practices have been twisted, maligned and often perverted by subsequent religious power brokers through the decades, centuries and millennia of religious-social-political-economic upheaval and change.

This is why we turn to God. This is why you must

strive to move outside your Triangle and yourself, to reach God as you struggle through life's lessons. When you make God the "hub" in your "wheel of life" the spiritual connection of your spokes to your hub brings you the strength, integrity and balance you need, which gives direction. When your spirituality is directly connected to the Lord and He is the hub of your wheel, it is He who helps you to hold together the spokes of your life to be as close to perfection and balance as possible.

So what about your tire? You can't ride endlessly on your rim without abrasion, discomfort and injury. How do you attain a comfortable and cushioned element between yourself and the potholes and ruts of your path? What makes up this buffer element of your tire?

This is where the object of your faith comes into play. If you allow God to be the hub of your wheel by putting in place and constantly adjusting your spokes in relationship to Him, you have only to add the last single element that allows all the parts of your wheel to be joined together and interact coherently. The followers of each religious belief system look to the one who holds for them this esteemed position. Each belief system has one to whom its followers turn and emulate. It is he who spiritually completes them.

For the Christian, this is Jesus. His words, teachings and examples aid the Christian in traveling the rough path of life that may lie ahead. It is only through Jesus Christ that one can hone the ability to absorb the bumps and bruises along the way and know that no matter what obstacles may appear to test the mettle of rim and spokes, the wheel will remain intact. As you travel the path of your life, between your belief in God and your faith in Christ, the rim and spokes of your being will remain strong and balanced.

CHAPTER 7

Laws
(Natural, God's and
Man Made)

God created and put into place the laws of nature to ensure balance in the natural universe. The natural laws of both our world and the universe are indisputable. Although many may still be unknown to us, many others which have tremendous impact upon our lives have only recently been empirically and scientifically proven in the last few centuries. The more we learn about our planet and its place among the stars and other celestial bodies, the more knowledge about our place in the universe is revealed.

The difference between the laws of nature and the laws of man may be as great as the difference between our macrocosmic universe and our microscopic world. In a perfect world each of us would live righteously and coexist amicably. If that were the case there really wouldn't be much necessity for us to be here, going through the lessons of this life. The fact is we are here, our lives can be difficult and there is much for each of us to learn and practice along the path.

People have lived for thousands of years by oral and written codes or laws and have depended upon them for judicial guidance. Societies have come up with volumes of laws, codes and codicils to govern and prescribe every consequence of behavior. As mankind developed and expanded from small groups and tribes into larger communities, codes of behavior and punishment were implemented to guide people in and through their lives. Evidence of these can be seen in artifacts from various cultures around the world. One of the oldest physical records to be found is the Babylonian "Code of Hammurabi" a written collection of laws in use circa 1750 BCE.[1]

These types of empirical legally binding codes as well as a variety of other similar local and ethnic collections of common law have been used in the Middle East region for millennia.

All of the world's major religions and spiritual belief systems also have written and recorded documents detailing their histories and legal proclamations. It is upon these writings that followers and group adherents base their beliefs and actions in daily life situations (or so they claim).

In this same way God gave the Judeo-Christian communities His Ten Commandments. As we have seen they address for us virtually every moral and ethical situation we may find ourselves in.

Everything we need to know and understand in living with the Lord and with each other is encapsulated in them. As we have learned in our own lives however, as easy as the Lord may have made things, we each manage to make our lives more complicated.

Although considered to be a foundation, men of legal councils and legislatures have transformed God's Ten Commandments into volumes of civil and criminal applications, becoming laws details. It is interesting that we place our faith in thousands of manmade prescriptions yet find it difficult or refuse to live by God's Ten Commandments.

For many the Ten Commandments have given rise to thousands of laws by which governments have gained and/or been given control over virtually every aspect of life. A plethora of laws has grown from the Ten Commandments for both the Jew and the Gentile, all written down for us, lest we forget.

For the Jews, legal documents and volumes began within the sacred Torah and its adjunct documents. For the Muslim, it began in the pages of the Quran and for the Christian, God's inspired words of law are found in the writings of the Bible, both Old and New Testaments. It is out of each of these that many corresponding individual societies and groups have developed civil and criminal statutes. While we put our faith in the massive collections of these works, it's both amazing and shameful that we have so much trouble with the simple morality of the original Ten Commandments.

What about the Bible? Let's start with the name

"Bible." It has been said that its letters stand for "Basic Instructions Before Leaving Earth." The Christian would be wise to take a look at, learn and live by these instructions.

On the surface the Bible can be a fairly daunting book to tackle. It has words, names, places and concepts that we may not be familiar with in our modern times, thus making our reading or study endeavors excruciatingly difficult and foreign.

Many people have asked such questions as "How should I read the Bible?" "Where do I start?" "What should I be looking for?" "How do I get past all the sections that are so boring or have so little to do with my life?" "What is the Bible really all about?"

Today you can choose from many different Bible editions and translations, one or more for practically any particular Christian interest group or persuasion. You can also choose from many different ways to read and study the Bible depending upon how "abridged or unabridged" you wish your efforts to be and what exactly you want to get out of your Bible. However no matter which publication or edition you choose, the focus of every Bible is always the same.

What is the Bible all about? In a word: Jesus. Yes, both the Old and New Testaments are about Jesus. The Old Testament is a history of God's promises and relationships with men and women over great periods of time and of the patriarchs, the tribes of Israel, Palestine and the Middle East. The New Testament is a history and testimony about the coming of Jesus as the Christ and the growth and development of the foundations of Christianity in the first century. However, the focus of both Testaments is on Jesus Christ.

Again, there are different ways to read a Bible depending upon what you are trying to accomplish. The Bible can be read as most other books are, beginning at page one. It is also possible however to read it in sections and parts, thematically, by a variety of categories, peoples, places or events or as an individual reader wishes.

The unabridged way would be to simply start at the beginning and go, but as mentioned, the Bible's complexities sometimes make it difficult to actually see relationships and how they have relevance today or how they may affect our lives. For a new believer or neophyte Christian looking for information on beginning his or her Christian walk, several other options are available. Depending upon your interests and needs, here are a few suggestions:

1. Read the New Testament Gospels: the books of Matthew, Mark, Luke, and John. The first three are known as the Synoptic Gospels for they tell the same basic stories, incidents and parables from the points of view of three different authors. Generally speaking these three give a presentation of Jesus' ministerial life and events.

2. Read the book of John (the fourth Gospel). This book relates more about Jesus and His spiritual ministry than any other book in the

Bible. Whereas the previous three Gospels talk in terms of Jesus' teachings, sayings and parables, the book of John explains more about Jesus' relationship with us as believers.

For a "one-time shot" reader, if you were going to read only one book in the Bible this would be the one.

3. Now for an excellent abridged version. If you own a red-letter edition Bible (that is, one in which Jesus' words are printed in red), this is a way you can approach your reading and study. For your first encounter, read only the words spoken by Jesus (the red words) and skip everything else in between. This may sound a little disjointed and as if it might not flow well but other than in a few places where a single sentence or only a few words are spoken, this method will give you a great overview. A foundation of Jesus' thoughts, words and deeds can be built and your initial spiritual relationship with Him quickened by this method. Through these red-letter words, His purposes, roles, life, death, resurrection and ascension, as well as the essential and important ideas and concepts of Christianity are all described and presented. In this way the basics you need to have a living relationship with Christ will become evident.

4. If you desire to know more about the early Christian movement, its spread throughout the known

world of the day or its early foundations upon which much of Christianity today relies, you might spend some time in following books as well: Acts, Romans, Hebrews and First and Second Corinthians. Written primarily by the Apostle Paul and addressing important issues for any new Christian, these books present applications of faith and belief that remain as relevant today as they were for those who wondered and struggled two thousand years ago.

5. Jesus' own "Cliff's Notes."

Two of the primary reasons Jesus came to earth were to give us glimpses of God's true character and nature and to be our example of how to live and experience more Christ-like (Christian) lives. God must have known that we would stray far away from Him in our selfish and busy lives because Jesus makes an effort to give us a living overview in a few dozen sentences.

Remember those days when you were in school and your teacher would be lecturing on a particular subject? As you busily took notes or doodled, all of a sudden your ears perked up and you tuned back in to hear the instructor say "Now take this down, because it will be on the final exam!"

That's exactly what Jesus has done for us in the New Testament. As He talks and teaches, there are instances when He says to us "OK everyone, listen up because this is important." These are some of the thoughts, ideas and concepts we need to be paying attention to and learn so we will have a better understanding of what our actions in this life are about. These are encapsulated for us in five words that Jesus uses over and over throughout the Gospels. These five words are: "I tell you the truth."

Examples: "I tell you the truth, whatever you did for one of the least of these brothers of mine, you did for me."[2] "I tell you the truth, no sign will be given to it [this generation]."[3] "I tell you the truth . . . no prophet is accepted in his hometown."[4] (In other versions and editions of the Bible, the phrase "I tell you the truth" is presented in different forms, usually termed "'Assuredly' 'Truly' or 'Verily' I say to you").

What do these words "I tell you the truth" mean? In the New Testament Jesus speaks to us in a succinct manner so that we may find the answers we need today. With His words "I tell you the truth" Jesus calls our attention to these statements of importance. He uses this phrase so that we might have all we need at any moment and not one thing more than necessary to live obedient and blessed lives. It is with these few statements that Jesus gives us the answers to many of the questions of our "final exam." In this way even for the most biblically sheltered of us, God in His infinite wisdom has made having a living relationship with Him very easy.

If we have no interest in the prose, poetry and verbiage of the Bible we can struggle, we can complicate and we can make our lives as complex and untruthful as we wish. It is we ourselves who have made our journey and relationship with the Lord difficult as we mire ourselves in our own deceits and with our own devices.

That may be our way but it is not the Lord's way. From the Ten Commandments of the Old Testament to the teachings of Christ in the New Testament, God has made our path to Him one of ease and understanding if we will simply be still and listen.

Exactly what is the truth? The truth is the truth, one hundred percent. Something cannot be ninety-nine percent true and one percent false and still be the truth. When it comes to truth, it is all or nothing.

How can we trust in and believe a person who speaks words he claims to be true? For the believer, God is truth[5] and cannot lie.[6] For the Christian believer, Jesus of Nazareth, the Christ has the authority to say the things He said regarding truth.[7]

As with God Himself, Jesus the Christ, the Son of God, indwelled with the Holy Spirit of God, cannot and would not lie. By His very nature being holy, as God is holy, Jesus is bound by the truth in thought, word and deed.

In our busy lives today with so many people, places and things vying for our attention it is easy for us to stray from the truth. Why is this? The truth has become a blur masked in the camouflaged landscape of our reality. Veiled by layer upon layer of life, the truth becomes harder and harder for us to find and execute as an integral part of our daily experiences.

When and where can we go to find the foundation of truth by which we may live? We will find the truth when we are ready to look for it and we will know where to look when we turn back to God's words. Be it in the Torah, the Quran or the Bible, God speaks to all who have ears to hear.[8]

What is the power of truth in your life? Freedom. If an individual is authentically bound by truth he or she cannot and would not deceive another, no matter the situation or circumstance. How much further down the path of life we would be if we understood the authority and raw power of "know the truth and the truth will set you free" [9] instead of sheepishly mumbling "I did it because I didn't want to hurt his/her feelings"

In the best interest of society as a whole we adhere to the thousands of civil laws and codes, written and imposed upon us. In our best interests, God through His written Word has provided us with twelve moral commands and four dozen codicils. The New Testament statements beginning with "I tell you the truth" are the Old Testament Ten and New Testament Two in action.

The Bible has a wealth of information for us to digest and understand if we wish to dig deeper. As is often the case with God however, less is more.

Endnotes

[1] Alfred Hoerth, *Archaeology and the Old Testament* (Baker Books, 1998), p. 119.

[2] Matthew 25:40.

[3] Mark 8:12.

[4] Luke 4:24.

[5] Psalm 31:5: "O Lord, the God of truth."

[6] Hebrews 6:18: "It is impossible for God to lie."

[7] Matthew 7:29: "He taught as one who had authority, and not as their teachers of the law."

[8] Mark 4:23: "If anyone has ears to hear, let him hear."

[9] John 8:32.

CHAPTER 8

God's Presence (the Kingdom of God)

Over the thousands of years of human history, technology has changed and therefore so has our world. During that same time span however, not much has changed in our behaviors and attitudes toward each other. What we have learned about each other has been passed down and taught generation after generation. Most of it has been by trial and error or by simple repetition.

In and through this passing of time, where is God to be found? In a church or cathedral? In a synagogue, mosque or temple? Is God here now, or should we not expect Him until the cataclysmic end times or apocalyptic last days? Where exactly is God?

For those who look for God in the past; history and archeology show evidence of His intervention. For those who look for God today, His presence is all around us to accept and revere. And for those who wish to wait on God's appearance in the future, they won't be disappointed for His words tell us of His impending arrival. We can acknowledge any one of these three states of being in time and space as the foundation of our belief or we may choose to miss it altogether.

Has God ever been here? It's amazing how many leaders, thinkers, teachers and philosophers have traveled the paths over the millennia. Of all those countless numbers who have been here, there was one who in three short years changed the lives of many people. Not only people of his day but also many more in the days, years and centuries to follow.

Many of those who lived at the time of Jesus, some two thousand years ago, were much like we are today; struggling, wondering, doubting, frustrated and somewhat confused about the world in which they lived. The followers of Jesus of Nazareth and His teachings were men and women, Jew and Gentile, young and old, well off and poor, learned and not, citizens and aliens. To each He spoke the same words, taught the same lessons and walked the same path of living examples.

The tensions that existed for the hearers of Jesus' teachings about the kingdom of God produced a myriad of emotions and misinterpretations. Even today much of what Jesus had to say falls on deaf ears or is rejected outright from mildly to violently. Jesus' comments and teachings were veiled in parables and questions. Rather than boldly pronouncing the answers from on high as in a tele-vangelist diatribe and display of self-righteousness, Jesus posed situations and questions for His audiences. Jesus invited His listeners to hear and then decide for themselves so that they might see through the tensions and emotions of this veil if they truly desired to discover the actions and concerns of a loving God.

For many what Jesus said was totally irrelevant. For most however what He said about God's presence and kingdom was simply confusing and misunderstood. We are overwhelmed and full of questions. Seekers from the world over still search to find the path that leads to God. Today more than ever before, many are thirsting for love and hungry for the truth.

Where can you go to find the presence of God? Many look to the masters who have been here and seek the opportunities to change themselves and thereby change their world. For the Christian believer the presence of Jesus both proves and validates the presence of God's kingdom in the past, present and future. By experiencing Jesus the veil is both lifted and drawn closer. Those who have the fortitude to look through the veil to find the Son will also find the opportunity, the example, the means and the way.

Once discovered Jesus asks us when we will choose to act upon our beliefs. And He demands an answer. He wants us to exercise our free will within our desire to discover Him, His Word and what a relationship with Him actually looks like on a daily basis. Jesus demands that His listeners make a choice and take action, as no one knows when the last breath and the last day may be. For each and every one of us our future will be our present sooner than not.

Balance is the essence and the natural state of existence. In all realms and possibilities of life, God and therefore His presence (His kingdom) always has and always will exist, for God is omnipotent,[1] omniscient[2] and omnipresent.[3]

His presence is in all He has created. The further we travel on the path with God, the more His Word will bring about a deeper, more complete sense of presence, understanding and peace to the lives of believers.

Endnotes

[1] Having unlimited authority or influence.

[2] Having infinite awareness, understanding, and insight.

[3] Present in all places at all times.

Part 3
Perception

"Everywhere is within walking distance
if you have the time."
—*Steven Wright, comedian*

CHAPTER 9

Jesus
(and Other Masters)

God does not need us to verify His existence. Neither are we necessary to validate His holiness. We on the other hand do need Him to validate the reason for our existence; otherwise we would have no reason for being here. The one plausible answer to the long-asked question of "Why are we here?" is for each of us to know and understand that God lives, that He exists, that He is.[1]

We often forget or have never realized that *all* people are worthy of God's love, for His love is un-conditional. How then can we be worthy of God's love enough to have a personal relationship with Him, yet still be unworthy to be in His presence?

We are in fact not worthy to be in His presence, for He is holy and we are not. God's holiness prevents us from being in His presence. He is also prevented from directly being in ours without the mediation of His Spirit in our lives. It is only through a mediator, that we as regenerated spirits after this life will ultimately be able to be presented to God. Jesus the Christ is that mediator.

The blessing planned for the believer of God's Word is everlasting life, with and in the presence of Almighty God after death.[2] For the Christian, it is through belief in Jesus of Nazareth as the Christ, and in His roles of savior and redeemer of our souls, that ensures we will be called through grace to a place of everlasting life in heaven.

God has communicated with us so that we may better know Him and ourselves. If we are true believers, we put our faith in the Lord's words.[3] In looking at God and His Word we find statements that actually have two separate yet interconnected meanings. First God has spoken to us through teachers, prophets, scriptural writings and miracles all pertaining to His Word and His will. There is however a second and even much more important connotation of God's Word for Christians. It is the manifestation of God's Holy Spirit, God's Word in human form, in the nature of the man Jesus of Nazareth. Christians hold to the writings of the Bible as being true where they pertain to this man. Based on the eyewitness testimonies, stories and biographical accounts from people who knew Jesus personally as well as those who lived and traveled with and were taught by him, Christians believe that He, Jesus was the incarnation of God in human form, that is, the Son of God.

His pre-existent place with God and His initial human manifestation can be concisely found in the book of John (1:1-2) as Jesus is described to us as being "in the beginning." "In the beginning was the Word, and the Word was with God and the Word was God."[4]

"The Word." It is easy for us today to identify each other and the things of our world because we all have names and have labeled or named the physical things of our existence. What name would you give to someone who pre-existed everything that we are aware of? God has existed forever. It is for this reason that John, the first-century disciple and apostolic writer initially identifies God for us as "the Word." "In the beginning was the Word [God]." In this way, we have a concept of His existence in a preeminent form that can be communicated to us in and through language (the "Word") we understand. People from every tribe, group, religious or spiritual system recognize God's preexistence in some form or fashion. Although there are many different names or labels for the entities identified as "God," He Himself has no need to have a name. It is only for our purposes and understanding that we have identified Him with a name. As John describes for the reader of the Bible, "In the beginning was the Word."[5] God is "the Word."

In the next part of the sentence, we are told of the existence of God's Spirit. "And the Word was with

God." Not only is God "the Word" but the total and eternal essence of God's Spirit is also "the Word."

It is God's Spirit who became incarnate as Jesus. Therefore, Jesus is also part of God's initial and forever existent Spirit.

As John says "And the Word was with God." Jesus is also with God as "the Word;" spiritually.

"And the Word was God." God was the Word, His Spirit was the Word and Jesus as "the Word" was God; therefore, "the Word"—Jesus—is and was God.

"He [Jesus; "the Word"] was with God in the beginning."[6]

"The Word became flesh."[7]

This next sentence of John's description of "the Word" relates the reason Jesus is our connection to God. These next sentences further describe for us the eternal existence of the essence of God that would become manifest in the flesh. (The "him" referred to is the incarnation of God's Spirit we know as the man Jesus).

"Through him all things were made; without him nothing was made that has been made. In him was life and that life was the light of men."[8] It is through this earthly flesh manifestation that we are given the explanation of God's Spirit in the man Jesus. The Father, the Spirit and Jesus are "the Word" and therefore God.

Sound confusing? Perhaps. Let's quickly recap: God is God. The essence of God (His Spirit) is God.[9] God and His Spirit (an existing and forever lasting

154

essence) are "the Word." Jesus (the name by which we as Christians know God's Spirit in the form of human flesh) is also "the Word". Jesus is God incarnate; Seed (man) of Mary and Sprit of God.

For the Christian believer God is found in a holy existence as the Trinity or triune Godhead (a united three-person nature). This means that the essence of God exists for the Christian as a three-person entity. God the Father; from whom we are separated. God the Son (Jesus); our bridge or connection and our way to the Father. And God the Spirit; who lives and dwells within the Christian through belief and faith in Jesus as the Christ. As Christians who trust the Holy Bible as God's inspired words and recorded teachings, God's Spirit is therefore part of our being. To be a Christian is to believe in the deity of Jesus of Nazareth as the Christ and to be His follower. Many Christians believe that Christ's thoughts, words and deeds are the examples to be used in the actions of their daily lives.

Many masters throughout the history of the world have been chosen men of God to whom He has talked directly and who have been commissioned to share God's words with others.

Virtually all peoples in the world today believe in one God or ultimate higher source, power, cosmic spiritual ideal or thought of the universe. It is highly probable that there are no longer any indigenous peoples on the planet today who have yet to come into contact with the outside world. As has been seen previously throughout modern history, all tribes and groups have innately worshiped one primary god, even in instances when they have multiple lesser deities such as representative elements of nature.

Focusing on the world's people with whom we are most familiar, it would appear that all are aware of the existence of God. If all have an understanding of God, what are the differences among them and their beliefs and why is there so much turmoil among us? The observation to follow is brief and cursory, to say the least. The comparisons and contrasts between belief systems are too numerous to address here. Having looked at these major religions in more detail in Chapter 5, for our purposes, we will now focus on two fundamental points: (1) the major similarity among all and (2) the major difference among all.

The quick answer to the first question is that they all believe in a god or supreme spiritual thought identity of the universe. The answer to the second is just as simple; only Christians believe that Jesus of Nazareth was the Christ, the Son of God incarnate.

Is Jesus truly the Son of God? Is He really God incarnate? Was He really God manifested in the flesh? Why does the Christian believe this to be so, especially when so many people throughout time and history have doubted and questioned Jesus' authenticity? This one sticking point has drawn people all over the world into discussions, debates and wars for centuries. It is the difference in the applications of God's words through Jesus that continues to often bring Christians and others to flash points and conflict.

Having identified the similarity among all belief systems, religions and sects (the existence of God or a supreme spiritual thought) and the main difference between them (the contention that Jesus of Nazareth was/is the Christ [Messiah]), perhaps the most interesting aspect is the similarity of basic philosophies and tenets between oral teachings and original written records. How can believers be so fundamentally close and yet at the same time be so far from each other in practice?

Each of the various sects or religious movements has had one primary leader who set the initial agenda, stage and provincial principles of its fundamental beliefs to be adhered to by its followers and group members. For Christians that person is Jesus. This is important for many men and women of God have been given words and instructions or have received inspired enlightened thought. Examples include Mohammed (Islam), Siddhartha Guatama (Buddha, Buddhism), Confucius (Confucianism), Lao Tse (Taoism), Bhranji Krishna (Hare Krishna), as well as the many Old Testament prophets, leaders and New Testament Judeo-Christian teachers, disciples and apostles. All of these people were masters, philosophers, teachers and religious/spiritual leaders and many were prophets of God or godly thought. All had early followers and groups of believers and many have large collections of disciples today.

So who was this man Jesus? And what's the big deal? Each religion or organized sect believes that its founder, leader or originator is God's one and only or at least God's foremost prophet or messenger. Every group of believers has one in whom they believe and follow fundamentally. Which master teacher, philosopher or spiritual leader was in fact God's select? Who really is *the one*? If we all believe in God, but don't agree upon the messenger, then who was God's chosen one? Which one is it?

It's every one of them.

Each was chosen to be a messenger of God and of His thoughts and words. Each believed and espoused similar tenets of civil, moral and ethical behavior. Each is recognized as a prophet or teacher of God's words.

However, only Jesus claimed to be and was said by others to be; the Son of God, the Christ (the Messiah),[10] the human manifestation of God[11] and God's Spirit in the flesh.[12]

Other than Jesus, not one of the other masters ever claimed to be the Son of God or God incarnate (in the flesh). Why not? Being men of truth, they couldn't, because they weren't.

Jesus was human. He was like you and me. He had good days and bad days. He was tempted, tried and tested, just as we are. He sometimes wondered, just as we do. He sometimes asked, just as we do.

How do we know who Jesus really was and is? And why should we believe Him, or believe in Him? These two questions are two sides of the same coin.

If we believe Him, then we believe everything He said and did was true. Therefore we know that He is who He claimed to be. If we believe in Him, then His words and actions are our validation that all ever said about Him is also true.

If on the other hand we do not believe, then nothing in His words, actions, thoughts or deeds will convince us otherwise.

What proof do we have that Jesus was and is who He claimed to be? Volumes are available in libraries and bookstores answering this question in detail. To tackle it here would make our steps much too complicated. The evidence is overwhelming that proves that Jesus was and is who He claimed to be. Suffice it to say that if we look objectively at the historical Jesus, His life and His ministry, there is more than enough evidence to make a case for belief, if we so choose. For those who refuse to believe the recorded evidence, then little would be convincing enough to overcome their doubts.

So how do we know that Jesus of Nazareth is the true Son of God? For the Christian, those who came before Him testified as to who He was.[13] God Himself testifies as to who Jesus is.[14] Jesus testified to us as to who He is.[15] And those who came after Him have testified about who He was and is.[16] For the Christian, the only way to eternal and everlasting life is through Jesus the Christ.[17]

What's the alternative to believing or not believing in Jesus? Do we believe and have eternal life[18] or not believe and, what?

159

What are your options when you pass from this reality? Everlasting life, death, hell, reincarnation? Yes, at least one of these, possibly more.

Each of us must decide for ourselves and make up our own minds as to who and what we will believe in and what we will trust to be the truth. This is one of the great aspects of God's love for us; that He allows each to believe whatever we might wish to without interference. God wants us to come to Him through His Son of our own accord, through our own volition and on our own path and choosing. In this way God is assured that we are with Him because we want to be.

As mentioned before, because God is God, He is holy and we are not, there is no way we can ever be with God or in His presence on our own or because of any particular thing we may have said or done.

Yes, we are able to recognize God for who He is. Yes, we are able to worship and praise God for being the holy one of the universe. We may even be able to agree with each other there is only one true and supreme God. All of these however do not lessen our distance from Him or serve the purpose of bringing us to Him. Only one man fulfilled that purpose. Jesus' role was to be our mediator, our way to come into God's presence and to be one with Him.

Each of history's masters, living or dead, past or present, teacher or preacher, from Abraham to Zoroaster tells us of God's magnificence, words, commandments, laws and ethics. However the only one who claims to be one with God in Spirit eternally is Jesus. Not one of the others from A to Z is willing to or able to make such a claim about himself.

Was Jesus of Nazareth the man, also the Son of God? Or was He just another Jewish prophet? We each believe in someone or something. The truth is you may believe anything you choose.

Why should you believe Jesus and what He says? Knowing what you now know are you willing to risk your entire eternal existence on *not believing* in Jesus as the Christ?

Endnotes

[1] Hebrews 11:6: "To please God . . . anyone who comes to him must believe that he exists."

[2] John 6:40: "For my Father's will is that everyone who looks to the Son and believes in him shall have eternal life."

[3] Matthew 4:4: "Man does not live on bread alone, but on every word that comes from the mouth of God."

[4] John 1:1.

[5] John 1:1.

[6] John 1:2.

[7] John 1:14.

[8] John 1:3–4

[9] John 4:24: "God is spirit."

[10] Mark 8:29: "You are the Christ."

[11] John 1:18: "No one has ever seen God, but God the One and Only, who is at the Father's side, has made him known."

[12] Mark 1:24: "I know who you are [Jesus of Nazareth]—the Holy One of God!"

[13] Micah 5:2: "Among the clans of Judah, out of you will come for me one who will be ruler over Israel."

[14] Mark 1:11: "And a voice came from heaven: 'You are my Son, whom I love.'"

[15] John 4:26: "I who speak to you am he."

[16] Colossians 2:9: "For in Christ all the fullness of the Deity [God] lives in bodily form."

[17] John 20:31: "Believe that Jesus is the Christ, the Son of God, and that by believing you may have everlasting life in his name."

[18] John 3:36: "Whoever believes in the Son has eternal life."

CHAPTER 10

Relationships (Plans and Paths, Not Buildings)

We have examined the interpersonal connection between God and Jesus, between God and others, and between God and us, so what does all this mean, and what is the "bottom line"? The bottom line of life is this: Relationships.

John Donne wrote, "No man is an island."[1] We are not here alone, we do not live isolated and alone, and we cannot exist alone. Even Jesus, the most alien, isolated and different man of all time, was never alone. He was connected to family, friends, followers, even foes, but always to God his eternal and heavenly Father and to the Holy Spirit.

Jesus acknowledged and accepted the role for which He had been brought to earth. He fulfilled the scriptures and promises that had been made about

Him throughout spiritual and religious history. Jesus told us once and for all that He is the way to eternal and everlasting life[2] in a prayer that He prayed before His arrest. It is here that we see the true relationship between Jesus the obedient Son and God, the guiding loving Father. Jesus said, "Father, the time has come. Glorify your Son, that your Son may glorify you. For you granted him authority over all people that he might give eternal life to all those you have given him. *Now this is eternal life:* that they may know you, the only true God and Jesus Christ, whom you have sent. I have brought you glory on earth by completing the work you gave me to do. And now, Father, glorify me in your presence with the glory I had with you before the world began."[3]

There is only one God and there was only one Son who was sent to earth by God the Father for the specific purpose of redemptive salvation. When we recognize, glorify and honor Jesus as the Christ, we recognize, glorify and honor God Himself through the Son He sent. In this way we gain the mediator we need, so that one day we will be able to stand in God's holy presence.

God is not exclusively found in buildings, churches, temples, synagogues or mosques. He is found in the heart, mind and soul of the believer but only if the believer invites God in and makes a dwelling place for Him. If you as a believer live with God in your daily life here and now, you will be blessed. And when you are finally in His presence after this life, you will also be blessed to realize that your soul has been with Him from the beginning.

God had a plan for Jesus' life. He has a plan for your life as well.

When we obey God our lives become more fulfilling. As believers of God's Word we have nothing to fear, not even death. The sum total and purpose of our life comes down to one thought, one belief, one acknowledgement, one statement: "God, not my will, but yours be done."[4]

Life is about priorities and choices. What are yours? In every situation, choice or decision you must ask yourself: How will I respond? Will it be God's way, or my way?

Endnotes

[1] John Donne (1572–1631).

[2] John 14:6: "I am the way and the truth and the life. No one comes to the Father except through me."

[3] John 17:1–5 (emphasis added).

[4] Luke 22:42.

Epilogue

God has blessings for you, both here and here-after. He is waiting for you to decide, to choose and to act by becoming an obedient child of His today. No matter what you may have done, where you may have been or how many times you may have tried and failed, He is waiting with open arms, love and understanding.

If you ask, He will answer. If you stay on the path and follow the plan He has for you, your life will change, be blessed and never be the same. You will have more than you ever could have dreamed of or provided for yourself through your own efforts. It is never too late to begin or to begin again, a dynamic living relationship with God and His Spirit through His Son, Jesus Christ.

These things I know to be true, for I once was on a different path. However, this book is not about me. It's about God and you.

May you find God; Father, Son and Holy Spirit in your life, on you path and may there be a personal relationship between you and Him. He is ready when you are.

Mahalo Nui Loa. A Hui Hou.

May God bless and keep you, this day and all the days of your life.

~Branch Isole

Living on the island of Maui, Branch Isole shares God's Word and Mana'o* in writing and with individuals and groups visiting Hawaii.

Branch earned a Bachelor of Science teaching degree at Texas State University, did post graduate work at the University of Houston and holds a Master of Arts in Theology from Trinity Theological Seminary.

His catalogue of work includes poetry, short stories and articles for journals, magazines, newsletters and on the Internet at www.manaopublishing.com

Mana'o (pronounced Ma Na O)
is Hawaiian for Thoughts, Ideas and Opinions.

Other books by Branch Isole

Power of Praise ©
The Poetry of Spiritual Christianity
ISBN 0-9747692-7-4

Even Christians Stumble and Fall ©
Musings of a Struggling Believer
ISBN 0-9747692-4-X

Crucibles ©
Refinement of the Neophyte Christian
ISBN 0-9747692-3-1

Barking Geckos ©
Stories and Observations in Poetic Prose
ISBN 0-9747692-2-3

Seeds of Mana'o ©
Thoughts, Ideas and Opinions in Poetic Prose
ISBN 0-9747692-1-5

Reflections on Chrome ©
Parking Lot Confessions in Poetic Prose
ISBN 0-9747692-5-8

Postcards from the Line of Demarcation ©
Points of Separation in Poetic Prose
ISBN 0-9747692-6-6

Messages in a Bottle ©
Inspirations in Poetic Prose
ISBN 0-9747692-9-0

Saccharin and Plastic Band Aids ©
Comments in Poetic Prose
ISBN 0-9747692-8-2

To order any of these books, please visit:

MANAO PUBLISHING
www.manaopublishing.com

<u>NOTES</u>

www.ingramcontent.com/pod-product-compliance
Lightning Source LLC
LaVergne TN
LVHW011351080426
835511LV00005B/237